Walks to Wet your Whistle

*Circular walks, with a pub, in
Shropshire and along its
Staffordshire Borders*

by
Roger Seedhouse

Meridian Books

Published 1997 by Meridian Books

ISBN 1-869922-34-4

A catalogue record for this book is available from the British Library.

Meridian Books
40 Hadzor Road, Oldbury, Warley, West Midlands B68 9LA

Printed in Great Britain by MFP Design & Print, Manchester.

Contents

Introduction

Perceptions

When it comes to walking, attitudes vary enormously. Some would be filled with dread at the prospect of having to walk half a mile; others would regard a twenty mile trek as little more than a stroll. This publication is aimed at what is probably the vast majority of us who fall somewhere between these two extremes.

Pleasures

You've heard it before but I'll say it again – walking is good for you! It is an inexpensive way to get exercise and allows you to see at close hand the wonderful countryside with which this island is blessed. It is amazing how much hidden beauty there is even on your own doorstep – go out and enjoy it!

Pubs

A pub is not essential for a good walk but the two combine admirably together. Many walkers appreciate a watering hole *en route* or at the end of a walk – not extremely 'posh' pubs serving expensive meals (walkers don't tend to be popular in such places) but simple country locals where they can take a break and sample the unique character which some of them possess. However, there is no point in having a great pub and an indifferent walk, or vice-versa, and in striking a balance it is inevitable that there will be a mix of pub types, although I have endeavoured to confine the choice to those where the walker will feel at ease. It is an unfortunate symptom of modern times that many country pubs are struggling to survive and some find it to be not worthwhile opening during weekday lunch-times. Notes on individual opening times are given in the Factfiles, though I am unable to guarantee that there have not been any changes since going to press.

Points to consider

1. Wear sensible gear. A good pair of boots is essential; so are waterproofs and warm clothing in less clement weather or when undertaking wild hill walks.

2. If you can, take a map of the area. Landranger (1:50,000 or 1¼ inches to the mile) is the most commonly used but Pathfinder (1:25,000 or 2½ inches to the mile) with much more detail is better. I am not suggesting this because you are likely to get lost but merely as a prudent precaution just in case you do stray off the route or if, perhaps because of deteriorating weather, you want to cut short the walk. A compass is also a valuable item for the same reasons.

3. Some paths, particularly those less well used, can get overgrown in summer. A walking stick can make life a lot easier in such situations and, sometimes, a pair of secateurs. A small first aid kit should also be carried in the event of a close encounter with a bramble or other mishap.

iv

4. The countryside is constantly changing. Seasonal changes can make things which appear obvious or easy to recognise in summer less so in winter and vice-versa. Be wary also of physical changes. The position or type of gate/fence/stile may be altered, field boundaries are changed or even removed altogether, tracks can be diverted (officially or otherwise), etc.

5. Without wishing to state the obvious, give consideration to the choice of time to do a particular walk. Not the time of day necessarily, although you will need to allow adequate time to complete the main walks, but the time of year. You may wish to avoid those walks covering intensively farmed areas during, say, June – August when paths over cropped fields can be a problem. Even though landowners are under a legal obligation to maintain paths after planting, some of them don't. Similarly, I would not advise walking over very hilly country (The Stiperstones, for example) on an iffy winter's day. I have endeavoured to give some guide as to the best times to do the walks in each Factfile.

6. A Right of Way is precisely what it says – you have the right to walk along it at all times unimpeded. Fortunately, most County Councils pursue a continuing programme of clearing and waymarking paths, but this is a huge task and many remain obscure. Likewise, most landowners adopt an enlightened attitude towards walkers but occasionally obstructions will be encountered, paths will have been obliterated or diverted or not reinstated after planting has taken place. Try not to be daunted by such things and remember that you have a legal right to pass. Needless to say, common sense should come to the fore in such situations; for example, it may be necessary to take a path around the edge of a cropped field rather than across it or follow an unofficial diversion rather than stick to the line on the map. Any serious obstructions should, however, be reported to the local Council's Rights of Way department – addresses are given at the end of this introduction.

7. Some animals can create consternation for the walker. Farm dogs are frequently encountered but mostly make a lot of noise rather than cause any physical injury. Again, a walking stick is useful just to be on the safe side. A field of frisky young bullocks is best avoided. Even though they are merely curious or think you have come to feed them, I prefer to skirt around them where possible. Sheep are no problem!

8. Not many landlords like muddy boots trampling over their floors. Try to be considerate and, if you cannot clean them off, take them off and leave outside or in a lobby.

9. Last, but not least, **REMEMBER THE COUNTRY CODE!**

Enjoy the country and respect its life and work.
Guard against all risk of fire.
Keep dogs under close control.
Keep to public footpaths across farmland.
Use gates and stiles to cross field boundaries.

Leave all livestock, machinery and crops alone.
Take your litter home.
Help to keep all water clean.
Protect wildlife, plants and trees.
Make no unnecessary noise.
Fasten all gates.

The Walks

WITH one exception the shorter walks are contained within the route of the main walks and those paths applicable to short routes only are denoted by dots on the sketch maps.

Main walks are designed so that the pub break is roughly at the half-way point; shorter routes start and finish at the pub. *Individual circumstances may dictate a change of start point to fit in with public transport or pub opening times.*

Grid references (GR) for the starting points are given in the Factfiles. If you are unfamiliar with the use of these you will find details on Ordnance Survey Landranger maps.

Reference points on the sketch maps are shown in the text thus: **1**

Public transport services to some areas are very limited or even non-existent – see individual Factfiles for details. In a few cases there is a better service to the start of the shorter walk so, if you are going to do the main walk, you may prefer to start and finish at the shorter starting point. Although public transport details were believed to be correct at the time of going to press you should always check times before setting off. Some appropriate telephone numbers are:

> *British Rail: 0345 484950*
> *Centro (West Midlands trains and buses): 200 2700*
> *Severn Valley Railway: 0800 600 900 (Talking Pages)*
> *Shropshire Busline: 0345 056785*
> *Staffordshire Busline: 01785 223344*

County public transport timetables can be purchased. For details and current prices telephone:

> *Shropshire Public Transport Unit, 01743 253030*
> *Staffordshire Busline, 01785 223344*

Details of pub opening times are given in the individual Factfiles. Regrettably, some country pubs now find it necessary to close at certain periods, particularly weekday lunch-times, and this might cause some difficulty if you wish to walk on a weekday. In such cases we suggest that you might like to start at the pub and time your walk to take advantage of evening opening hours.

Other than at busy times, most landlords will not object to you leaving a car on their car park if you are going to visit the pub when you return, but if in any doubt please ask permission.

GOOD WALKING!

About the author

Roger Seedhouse is a Chartered Surveyor and a partner in a firm of property consultants in the West Midlands. He has lived on the border of Shropshire and Staffordshire all his life and has an extensive knowledge of both counties. When not ministering to the requirements of his two daughters his spare time is divided between Rotary Club activities and walking.

To my wife Lesley and our good friends Mike and Pat Wootton for their tremendous help in the preparation of, and research for, this book.

Thanks also for their assistance to the staff of both Shropshire and Staffordshire Councils' Rights of Way Departments.

If, when using this book, you find any obstructions or problems of access on rights of way it would be very helpful to report these to the appropriate local authority (and to Meridian Books).
The addresses are:

Shropshire:
Rights of Way Section
Leisure Services Department
Column House
7 London Road
SHREWSBURY SY2 6NW

Staffordshire:
Rights of Way Section
Department of Planning and
*   Economic Development*
County Buildings
Martin Street
STAFFORD ST16 2LE

Location Map

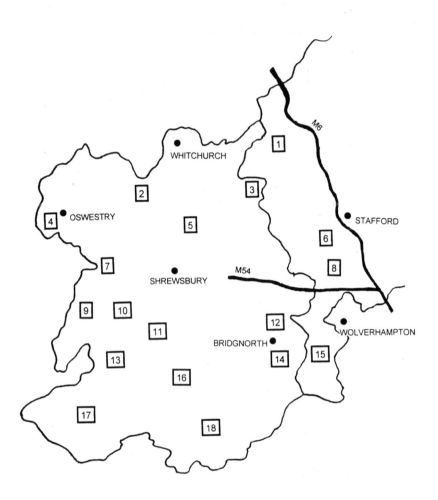

WHITCHURCH

1

2

3

OSWESTRY

4

5

STAFFORD

6

7

M54

8

SHREWSBURY

9

10

11

12

WOLVERHAMPTON

BRIDGNORTH

13

14

15

16

17

18

M6

Publishers' Note

Every care has been taken in the preparation of this book. All the walks have been independently checked and are believed to be correct at the time of publication. However, neither the author nor the publishers can accept responsibility for any errors or omissions or for any loss, damage, injury or inconvenience resulting from the use of the book.

Please remember that the countryside is continually changing: hedges and fences may be removed or re-sited; landmarks may disappear; footpaths may be re-routed or be ploughed over and not reinstated (as the law requires); concessionary paths may be closed. The publishers would be very pleased to have details of any such changes that are observed by readers.

1
Ashley

FACT*file*

MAPS: Landranger 127; Pathfinder 829

DISTANCES: 8¼ miles; shorter walk 3¾ miles

MAIN START: Car park at the crossroads opposite Broughton Parish Room on the B5026 at Wetwood, about four miles north-west of Eccleshall and three miles south-east of Loggerheads. GR774333.

> **Public Transport:** Very limited bus service 436 Stafford to Telford calls at Wetwood Crossroads (Tues only).

SHORT START (page 5): The Meynell Arms, Ashley, from the car park opposite. Ashley is approached from the B5026 via a turning three quarters of a mile south-east of Loggerheads or from the A53 about 1½ miles on the Newcastle side of Loggerheads. GR763366.

> **Public Transport:** Bus service X64 Shrewsbury to Hanley calls at Ashley.

TERRAIN: Interestingly variable through farmland and woods with loads of historical features. Gentle climbs only. Walkable at any time although a few paths may be overgrown or planted over in summer.

THE PUB: The Meynell Arms is an unpretentious local with bar and lounge, boasting a number of lesser known ales, e.g. Salisbury Ales with a religious flavour such as Bishops Tipple, Deacon and Wake Ale. Also Theakstons, Bass, Worthington, Guinness etc.

Food available at certain times including Sunday lunch. Closed Mon-Thurs lunch-times.

As an alternative on weekdays the Robin Hood at Jugbank (see map) is open at lunchtimes, except Mondays.

TURN left along the B5026 towards Loggerheads past The Old Vicarage and after around a third of a mile branch off left down a lane signed Fairoak. As you approach the turning you can see to the half right the magnificent Broughton Hall which, until recently, was a Franciscan monastery. It was described by Pevsner as 'the most spectacular piece of black and white in the county' and has quite a history which, unfortunately, space does not permit me to relate. It is reputed to be haunted by a ghost known as 'Red Socks'.

The lane bisects a fir wood, bears left and, as it comes out of the bend, turn right down a broad track to the left of a cottage. At a junction turn right towards Green Farm, then immediately left through a metal gate to follow the waymark sign leading onto a broad grassy farm track. After a while it becomes enclosed with hedgerows and then opens out again into a field where you pass a rather superfluous stile. However, immediately on your left is another stile in the boundary fence and, having crossed this, proceed on a narrow path between hedge and fence ignoring a further stile on the left after about 120 yards.

Cross a stile under an oak tree into a field keeping to the left down a narrow sunken path (which can get churned up) and go through a timber gate along a short section of farm track to cross another stile 20 yards ahead into the next field. Keep to the left hedged boundary as the way develops into a sunken track along the field edge. After a while you climb out of it and continue to follow the left boundary to the end of the field where you go through a metal gate. From here continue the same line forward on a track through the centre of a field with woodland to both sides.

The track is joined by a post and wire fence on the left bordering the edge of a pasture field and continues as it passes to the left of Goldenhill Farm. Cross the bottom of the farm driveway, through double metal gates and after another 150 yards turn right at a T-junction along a metalled surface. After another 125 yards or so there is a gateway into the field on your right. **1**

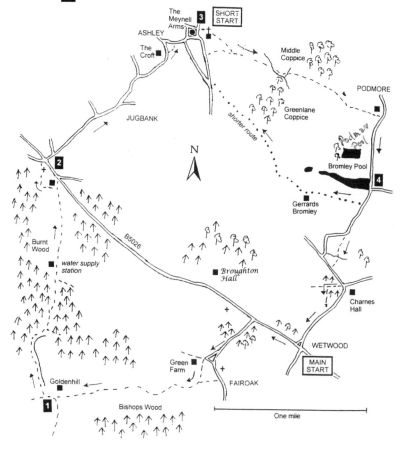

2

Go through the gateway keeping to the right field boundary, through another gate onto a track with a post and wire fence on your left and a brook on your right. This is an attractive section approaching the southern end of Burnt Wood and, at the field corner in front of the wood, cross a stile and turn right onto a narrow sunken path to follow around the right edge of the wood. The path climbs gently and after a while joins a broader track to enter Burnt Wood.

BURNT WOOD and BISHOPS WOOD *were once part of the great hunting forests which covered this corner of Staffordshire. The name 'Ashley' means a clearing in the ash woods and the villagers were obliged to provide assistance to the Bishop of Lichfield whenever he wished to hunt in the forests. Burnt Wood gets its name from charcoal burning and in the sixteenth century the burners supplied fuel to the Huguenots for the manufacture of glass in furnaces located in Bishops Wood before the industry moved to the Black Country. Both woods now belong to the Forestry Commission.*

A further short climb will bring you to a junction with a forestry road. Cross this directly onto the path opposite and continue a gentle climb ignoring all side paths. On meeting another junction bear right along the main track, again ignoring all side paths. As the wood ends the track narrows on its approach towards a small brick building ahead and exits through a metal gate onto a concrete driveway.

Go through double metal gates to follow the gravelled track to the right of the building, which in fact is the Severn-Trent Burntwood Water Supply Station. The surface changes to tarmac as it continues between fields for about a third of a mile and, just before reaching a bungalow on the left, cross a waymarked stile into a field. The official route is slightly left across the field to a stile in the opposite boundary but it may be more practical to follow the field edge around to the same point. Whatever, cross the stile turning right into another field to follow the mixed tree boundary and at the end there is another stile which leads onto a narrow path to the right of a large transformer station, which in turn exits via steps onto a lane in front of a tiny Victorian Providence Chapel. Turn right here to meet a junction with the B5026. **2**

Cross directly down Lower Road towards Ashley. Ignore all turnings off as the road continues for some time through the scattered semi-rural communities of Hookgate and Jugbank with their neat, well maintained houses and cottages. You will pass the Robin Hood Inn on the left, and just after a small cottage on your left named 'The Croft' take a public footpath on your right on the crown of a left hand bend. Ignore a stile on the right and follow the path to exit onto a lane. Turn right past the Spar shop and carry on the lane as it bears left around the church and the Meynell Arms is a further 100 yards or so on your left. **3**

ASHLEY. *Recorded in the Domesday Survey, the village of Ashley was once surrounded by large forests and heathland (see notes on Burnt Wood) and although still relatively unspoilt and semi-rural, some* *modern development has taken place in response to demand from commuters. Local family names are prominent, particularly Meynell and Gerrard and it is said that early in the eighteenth century the last of the Gerrard family staked his Ashley estates on a game of cards and lost to Littleton Meynell who became Lord of the Manor in his place – what a loser! The Church has a number of interesting features including the largest alabaster tomb in any parish church in the country, built in 1603 by the then Lord Gerrard. There is also a black basalt funerary urn made by Josiah Wedgwood in memory of his benefactor, Sir William Chetwynd.*

Don't be lulled into lethargy as there is still a way to go! On leaving the pub, take the footpath opposite alongside the left of a cottage and after 20 yards bear right at a fork and over a stile by a metal gate onto a grassy track. This track runs between fields and at the end of it you will cross another stile by a metal gate and yet another stile by yet another metal gate after what might be a muddy 20 yards between them.

Cross the ensuing field directly to reach, would you believe, a stile by a metal gate on the opposite boundary. Cross this and in the next field continue the line forward to the right of some electricity poles to gain the far side and a footbridge with stiles at each end. At the time of research the farmer had marked the path across the field but this may not always be there. Cross the footbridge and follow the direction sign right along the field boundary with a brook on your right, past an ornamental pool and continue to follow the boundary as it swings 90 degrees left at the corner of Greenlane Coppice.

After another 50 yards look for a stile and footbridge in trees on your right. Once over, bear half left across another field towards the front corner of Middle Coppice and, on reaching it, veer right to follow the front edge. Cross a stile by, yes, a metal gate and at the end of the wood is another gate and waymark post, after which bear very slightly right towards a clump of trees where there is a hollow and a pool. Pass to the right of the pool and then cross a stile on your left after 50 yards into a field and follow the left hedged boundary.

At the end is a stile level with farm buildings on your left; cross this and continue the line forward in the next field to another stile 50 yards ahead. I encountered a stock fence in front of the stile but don't let that worry you. Turn right onto a lane and walk along it over a bridge, ignoring a crossing right of way, until reaching Bromley Pool. On a fine day you might care to pause awhile at this pleasant spot. **4**

Continue on the lane for about another a quarter of a mile to where it turns sharp right. There is a waymarked stile in the hedge on your left – cross cutting off the right corner of the field (I had to walk around it because of crops) aiming to the right of a line of trees at the top. Here there is a little footbridge and a metal gate to negotiate into the next field where you bear very slightly right towards the right corner of a small fir wood ahead. Cross a stile onto a lane and turn left for 150 yards or so to reach

Bromley Pool

a T-junction in front of Charnes Hall – not so attractive as Broughton but shares with it the distinction of being haunted; in this case the ghost is called ' Silkie'.

Look for a stile in the hedge on the right leading into the small wood and follow the grassy path through it to a kissing gate on the far side. Once through the kissing gate bear half left across the field aiming just to the left of farm buildings to arrive at a double stile down to a lane. Turn right along the lane for about 400 yards to return to the starting point.

SHORTER WALK

FROM the Meynell Arms, point 3, follow the main route to Bromley Pool, point 4. Continue on the lane for about 200 yards and turn right through a gate along a waymarked path to the left of some cottages towards Gerrards Bromley. As the track swings left in front of the house, continue ahead through a timber gate and after a further 25 yards ahead again on the driveway to the house. The property is one of some distinction and has a number of unusual architectural features.

The driveway loops left around to the rear of some very old stone barns and almost opposite what appears to be an original stone built carriage entrance to a stable yard, bear right down a farm track and through a metal gate. I was somewhat intrigued by this carriage entrance and further investigation revealed a most fascinating history. It was in fact the entrance to Bromley Hall, described in Plot's *Natural History of Staffordshire* as 'the most magnificent structure of all this county' – the very same property gambled away by Digby Gerrard (see notes on Ashley). It was demolished by Littleton Meynell in 1750.

After about 75 yards you can see the end of Bromley Pool and the track swings left on a concrete drive alongside some silage stores. Immediately after these cut left through what will be the first of a number of swing gates and into a field. Don't follow the left boundary but gradually move away from it and, once over the brow, continue the line diagonally towards the bottom right corner of the field. The field drops down towards the corner and at this point you should bear right to go through another swing gate in the right boundary of the field, avoiding the temptation to cross the stile ahead right in the corner.

Having crossed the next field and gone through another swing gate in front of a copse, bear half left up a slight rise and through another swing gate into the next field. Continue line more or less straight forward towards a clump of trees in the distance, to the left of which is a swing gate. You are now at the junction of boundaries to three fields – go through the swing gate and diagonally opposite through a metal gate with a fence stile to the side of it to follow a marked path diagonally across the centre of the field, passing to the left of Greenlane Coppice.

At the end of this long field is a double stile leading into another field with some unusual topography. It is in fact a ridged field with the remains of a medieval farming method of dividing the land into strips for cultivation by individual villagers. Follow the waymark across with Ashley now in view off to the right. After about 100 yards at a more pronounced dip, which is probably the site of a grubbed up hedge, bear very slightly right across the remaining part of the field, passing to the left of a small hollow to the opposite boundary where you meet the hedged corner of the adjacent field. Here there is a gate; turn left through it and follow the hedged boundary for about 100 yards to a stile on your right. Cross this and bear half left to cut off the bottom left corner of a field to a stile in a hedge near to the top left corner. Cross and turn right onto a lane. After 50 yards keep right at a junction down Charnes Road and then bear right again a T-junction by the church and back to base.

The Meynell Arms

2
Colemere and Wem Moss

P ROCEED out of Welshampton on the A495 towards Ellesmere for about a quarter of a mile and take the first turning on the left down a narrow lane signed 'unsuitable for motor vehicles'. It is, however, extremely suitable for walkers and winds a quiet way over a crossroads after a third of a mile and continues towards Colemere with nice views on both sides over gently rolling countryside. Cross a footbridge over the 'Shroppie' and pass a gorgeous black and white thatched house with a large garden and its own private mooring.

After a further 20 yards bear left down a waymarked path into Boathouse Wood. This super path follows a course through attractive mixed woodland with views over Colemere which is, arguably, the best of all the Meres. I walked this route in autumn and the colours were brilliant.

See how many tree varieties you can spot – ten or more would be a reasonable score.

COLEMERE. *Iron age glaciers shaped the Meres which are now a haven for a variety of bird life. Colemere is the second largest and the edges are gradually being colonised by reeds and rushes. Snipe can be seen in the marshy area beyond the sailing clubhouse. It is also the only place in England where a rare type of water lily is found – more information about this and other things relating to the Mere can be found on a plaque which you will pass at the southern end.*

At the end of the Mere you pass through a gate by the period boathouse, which gives its name to the wood, and bear right up a path to exit onto a lane. **1**

Turn left here past the public car park (where the information plaque

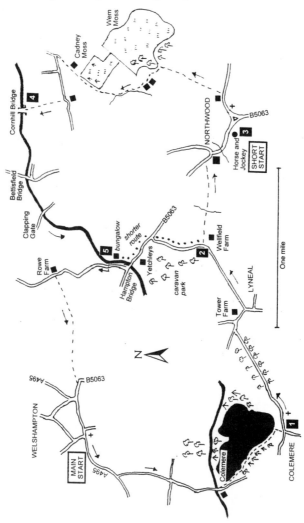

Avenue of horse chestnuts approaching Lyneal

is to be found) and St John's Church. The church was built in 1870 and has an unusual monument at the rear, a tall slender cross seven feet high supported by iron rods. You will next enter a long avenue of horse chestnut trees which must be a veritable paradise for the young in autumn. As you proceed along, horse chestnut give way to lime and you reach a T-junction.

Turn right into Lyneal, one of the oldest villages in Shropshire and containing a number of interesting buildings, including a pretty black and white cottage on the right called, fairly predictably, 'Rose Cottage' – real chocolate box stuff this one. Ignore a lane on the left, immediately after which comes Tower Farm with its unusual ornate chimneys. On meeting the next T-junction turn left and walk along a quiet lane for about half a mile until reaching Wellfield Farm. **2**

There is a waymarked, if somewhat dilapidated, stile to the left of the entrance drive to the farm which takes you into a short section of field. Cross this field before negotiating a crossing fence and continue in the next field to the left of a long barn towards the top right corner. Here there is a footbridge over a brook with stiles at each end and, having gone over, continue along the right-hand side of another field for 75 yards and cross a stile in the corner. From there continue your line diagonally across the adjacent field to a double stile close to the right-hand corner, just to the left of some farm buildings. *At the time of research this field was planted and I decided to pursue a course around the edge to the same point.* Cross the stiles onto a lane and turn right to follow through an S-bend into the village of Northwood and the Horse and Jockey on your right. **3**

Sooner or later you will have to extract yourselves from the comfort of the pub and turn right, then immediately left up a lane signed Whixall School. There is a curious chapel on the right with a plaque stating it to be a 'Primitive Methodist Jubilee Chapel' built in 1860. On passing a farm

9

on the left, bear left up a broad stone track which follows a pleasant trail for half a mile or so to reach the corner of a wooded area fringing Wem Moss. The track swings left in front of the trees, and a short diversion right over a footbridge will bring you to an information board about this, the latest of our National Nature Reserves.

WEM MOSS. *Administered by the Shropshire Wildlife Trust, Wem Moss is an excellent example of an increasingly rare lowland peat bog and rests on 12,000 years of plant remains which in some places are over six metres deep. The information board will tell you about the rare plants and wildlife which live there, including the great raft spider and white faced dragonfly. I did follow the path around to the edge of the bog and, although not actually coming across these things (and not really wanting to!) I found it to be a strangely atmospheric place*

Retreat back to the track and continue on past the driveway to a cottage, 2 Wem Moss, and stay with it as it kinks right to pass by another cottage. Immediately afterwards you will reach a further, larger, property which is right on the England-Wales border and it is here that I encountered the only slight difficulty on the whole walk (nothing to do with having crossed over the border I trust!).

You need to pass into the field to the right of the property but the way was fenced off with barbed wire. However I can assure you that this is an official right of way and, unless it has now been removed, you will have to negotiate the wire with care and follow the field edge to pick up a hawthorn line after the end of the house garden. A brook comes in from the left and you follow the right bank of it for about 250 yards until it kinks left to form a triangle with the path and here continue the line forward to meet the brook again and make for the wood ahead.

Go through a gate at the end of the field onto a grassy track along the left side of the wood, known as Cadney Moss. The trees end and if you look to the right you may see the remains of Bettisfield Windmill. At the end of the track is a former steam powered corn mill dated 1868 which, at the time of research, was in the process of conversion into what promises to be a most unusual residence.

Go forward on a tarmac lane and after about 250 yards turn left opposite Brook House and walk along a very straight bit of lane for a quarter of a mile or so. Where it bends left by a cottage, you cut right following a waymark into a field. Cross the centre of it in a straight line and pass through posts at the end to cross Cornhill Bridge, turning immediately left onto the towpath of the Shropshire Union Canal. **4**

A walk of some a third of a mile will bring you to Bettisfield Bridge (No.49) with a small marina and boatyard. Continue on the towpath under Clapping Bridge after which you enter a pretty section of the canal with quite good views in parts, although the surrounding countryside is fairly flat. Along this section you will cross back into England again and eventually come to a point where the towpath is joined on the right by a lane. After a short distance you will see a farm and bungalow on the opposite side of the canal and here look for a gate on your right giving access onto the lane and bear right onto it. **5**

You will pass a few cottages and continue through a long S-bend to arrive at Rowe Farm. Directly opposite is a gate and bridleway sign – turn left onto a path climbing through a field towards a group of trees on the horizon. Go through a gate at the top of the field onto a broad stony track between hedgerows which shortly opens out into another field. Follow the right boundary to join a gravelled drive in front of a cottage to exit onto the B5063. Turn right here and on reaching junction with the A495, bear left back into Welshampton.

SHORTER WALK

THIS shorter walk is a little longer than most but not too taxing. From the Horse and Jockey, point 3, follow the main route through to point 5 but do not go through the gate on your right onto the lane. Instead, continue on the towpath for a short while to reach Hampton Bank Bridge (No. 50). Here leave the canal to emerge through a gate onto the B5063 and turn immediately left to cross the bridge. Continue on the road passing Yetchleys Farm on the right and after a further 300 yards bear right along a lane signed Lyneal and Colemere. You will pass a residential caravan site on your right and shortly thereafter arrive at Wellfield Farm on your left, which is point 2. Cross the waymarked stile to the left of the entrance drive to the farm and follow the main route through to point 3 again.

The Horse and Jockey, Northwood

3

Knighton and Soudley

FACT*file*

MAPS: Landranger 127; Pathfinder 849

DISTANCES: 7¾ miles; shorter walks 3¼ miles, 4½ miles

MAIN START: The Wharf Inn, Shebdon which is situated on the Shropshire Union Canal about five miles north of Newport and 3½ miles west of Woodseaves. Parking is not that easy but there is a grass verge by the Wharf Inn frequently used by fishermen. GR758262. Alternatively, you could start from Soudley and break at the Wharf Inn.

> **Public Transport:** Nothing suitable other than an early morning (6.36 a.m.) Post Bus from Stafford, Mon-Fri, calling at Shebdon, returning at 4.16 p.m. (*But check with Busline.*)

SHORT START (page 16): There are two variations, one of which starts from the Wharf Inn, the other from the Wheatsheaf at Soudley, one mile south of Cheswardine, which itself is some five miles south-east of Market Drayton off the A529. GR726288.

> **Public Transport:** Very limited bus service 322 from Market Drayton (Wed only). Very limited service 439 from Stafford (Wed only) to Cheswardine, about half a mile from Soudley.

TERRAIN: Easy going through pleasant rural landscape with two stretches on the 'Shroppie' and an attractive wooded section. No climbs of any significance. Walkable at any time of the year although some fields on the section after The Wheatsheaf are likely to be planted in the summer.

THE PUBS: The Wheatsheaf is a typical village pub. It has an unpretentious bar (Poachers Retreat) and lounge (Squires Den) serving snacks and meals. Good selection of ales including Marstons, Banks's, Murphy's and Guinness. Also Tennants lager and Strongbow cider on draught.
Closed at weekday lunch-times.

The Wharf Inn: a pretty building with considerable character built during construction of the canal which passes above it along an aqueduct. Nooky interior having comfortable bars and restaurant. Beer garden. Offering a reasonable selection of house and guest ales.
Closed at lunch-times during the winter.

FROM the Wharf Inn walk towards the aqueduct bridge and after a few yards branch right up the embankment path. At the top turn left onto the towpath and over the bridge to walk along 'The Shroppie' for a distance of about three quarters of a mile.

You will arrive at somewhat of a blot on the landscape known as Knighton Works, which believe it or not is a Cadbury's factory. A strange place you might think for a chocolate factory but it has been here since the early part of the century! Indeed, it was then strategically located for the transport of its products by canal to the company's main plant at Bournville and it was as late as 1960 when use of canal boats for this purpose finally ceased.

Immediately after passing under the bridge by Knighton Works turn sharp left up the embankment to reach a road, turn left across the bridge by the factory and then immediately left again through a metal gate onto a path running along the top of the embankment. For the avoidance of doubt you should now be following a course on the opposite side of the canal to previously.

After 150 yards go through a waymarked metal gate to meet a track by the next bridge and cross the track diagonally to continue along the top of the embankment. The path winds through an area of scrub, which could become overgrown in summer, and then merges with the bordering field edge along which you walk until exiting onto another track by the next bridge. **1**

We now depart from the canal for a while. Opposite is a field and the way is diagonally across it to the opposite corner heading towards a wood. At the time of research the farmer had left a wide track marking the way but whether that was for the benefit of walkers or for his own convenience I don't know. (If the right of way is obstructed by crops it may be necessary to turn right on the track alongside and then left along a similar track by a small coppice to reach the same opposite field corner.) At

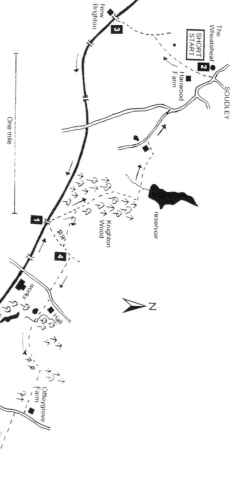

this point turn left through a waymarked gate.

The path you are now walking winds an attractive way through Knighton Wood and you will see considerable evidence of clearance and replanting having taken place. On passing through another waymarked gate proceed with the wood on your right along a grassy track and at the end of the wood turn left along a field edge with the southern end of Knighton Reservoir in view off to the right. This was the first reservoir to be built on the canal but was declared a failure in 1835 due to leakage and is now used simply for irrigation and fishing.

The path becomes quite narrow and descends through an area of sparse trees. Keep close to the left boundary and you will arrive at a footbridge and stile over a canal feeder brook. Cross and continue the line forward cutting off the bottom right corner of a field to meet a mixed tree boundary 30 yards ahead. Onward now with this boundary on your right and at the end of the field cross a stile.

The next field has a post and wire boundary on the right and you follow this around as it loops left to reach a stile to the right of a bungalow. Cross and pass to the right of the bungalow to a gate 20 yards ahead which exits onto a narrow lane. Turn right onto the lane and, on reaching a junction, turn right again. Ignore a turning right after 300 yards and continue into Soudley where you will find The Wheatsheaf quite easily. **2**

On prising yourself away turn right and after 30 yards, just before reaching a tiny Providence Chapel, cross a stile by a gate on your right. Walk along the left boundary of the field towards Hanwood Farm – don't be tempted to veer right along what might be a more obvious path around the rear of the buildings. At the end, cross another stile to continue the line more or less directly forward across the next field passing to the left of three trees to a further stile in the opposite boundary just to the left of an electricity pole.

Now bear very slightly right across the centre of the next field aiming about 50 yards to the left of a tree encircled pool towards the tree line on the far side. This field may be cropped in summer but the line is not critical and, on reaching the tree line, turn left in front of it along a broad grassy track. Continue to the bottom of a field where you pass through a dilapidated gate and bear half right across a short section of another field to meet a broad stony track. Turn left onto it for a short distance to arrive at a canal bridge in front of New Brighton Farm. **3**

Cross the bridge and turn immediately left down some steps onto the towpath. You will pass under three bridges, numbers 47, 48 and 49, before entering a peaceful straight section with Knighton Wood on your left and a steep embankment on the right. If, as I did, you choose a day when a fishing competition is in progress it may not seem all that peaceful particularly if you are obliged to step over or around countless fishing poles!

SHROPSHIRE UNION CANAL. *Engineered by Thomas Telford (who sadly died during its construction in 1834) 'The Shroppie' was* *the last great narrow boat canal to be built in England. Typified by deep cuttings and high embankments, it took 10 years to complete but never made a profit due to increasing competition from the railways. It was eventually taken over by London North Western Railway and fell into commercial disuse before the end of the last war.*

At the next bridge leave the towpath by going under the bridge and turning right up the embankment then right again over the bridge. You have now arrived again at point 1 on the outward route: branch left across the centre of the same field traversed earlier to the waymarked gate in the opposite corner. This time do not go through the gate but turn right onto a broad track, then left at a junction by a small copse and right a short distance further on at another junction. Continue for about a quarter of a mile to exit onto a lane. Turn left onto it but only for 50 yards before branching right through a timber gate to the side of an outbuilding to Knighton Hall. **4**

The Shropshire Union Canal

Follow the hedged boundary to the Hall with a fishing pool in view ahead and pass to the left of the pool to enter a track along the right edge of a copse. You will descend a short embankment and cross a plank footbridge which has seen better days and emerge into a field. Bear half left in the field, taking a course gradually moving away from the tree line on your right to reach a gap in a crossing boundary. You can see another pool off to the right through the trees. In the gap there is a waymark post concealed in the hedge directing you straight ahead to the left of a copse which comes into view and, on meeting the corner of it, proceed in the field with the copse on your right.

The trees shortly turn to hedge and on reaching a waymarked gate turn right and follow a track with a hedge on the left towards a small wood and

The Wharf Inn, Shebdon

Offley Grove Farm. Pass between wood and farm to meet a T-junction with the farm driveway. You can see at this point that the farm is a large complex converted into several dwellings. Continue forward on the driveway for a short distance to exit onto a lane.

Now, you can turn right here and walk along the lane for about half a mile back to the starting point but if you have any energy left the walk can be extended a little to finish with another canal section. To do this, turn right as directed but then bear left after 100 yards opposite gates to Offley Grove down a broad track between hedgerows. It narrows slightly and becomes grassy before exiting onto a lane.

Turn right and follow the lane for a little over a third of a mile to arrive at a bridge over the canal. Cross the bridge and turn right down steps onto the towpath. After another third of a mile you will come to the aqueduct from where the walk started – bear left down embankment and back to The Wharf.

SHORTER WALKS

THESE two alternative short routes together encompass almost the whole of the main walk.

For the longer route of 4½ miles start from The Wheatsheaf in Soudley, point 2, and follow the main walk through point 3 and along the Shropshire Union Canal to arrive at point 1. Having left the canal here proceed as for the outward route from point 1 through Knighton Wood back to the start.

The shorter alternative of 3¼ miles takes you from The Wharf as far as the road bridge by Knighton Works. Follow the main route directions for leaving the canal at this point but instead of bearing left along the embankment continue along the road in front of the factory for about a quarter of a mile to reach point 4 and the turning right through a timber gate to the side of an outbuilding to Knighton Hall. Now follow the main route back to The Wharf.

4
Offa's Dyke

FACT*file*

MAPS: Landranger 126; Pathfinder 847 & 827

DISTANCES: 9 miles; shorter walk 3½ miles

MAIN START: In the village of Treflach four miles south-west of Oswestry on the Nantmawr road, or approach from the south via the A495, turning right at Porth-y-waen for about 1½ miles (as you can tell we are very close to the Welsh border here). Parking in the village is restricted – there is a space by the bus stop on the way out towards Oswestry; alternatively you could park outside the Royal Oak Inn. GR259254.

　　Public Transport: Limited bus service D54 from Oswestry calling at Treflach.

SHORT START (page 22): From The Old Mill Inn at Tyn-y-coed, also approached from Oswestry via the Nantmawr road and a turning off it 2½ miles out of the town centre. GR255283.

　　Public Transport: Very limited bus service 454 from Oswestry (Wed only) calling at Pentreshannel a third of a mile south of Tyn-y-coed.

TERRAIN: Hill, vale, parkland, scenic views and a great section of the historic Offa's Dyke path. Walk at any time.

THE PUB: Although recently refurbished, The Old Mill Inn has retained its essential character and charm. An attractive period stone built property, it sits in delightful rustic surroundings in an isolated hamlet adjacent to Candy Woods and offers the visitor a wide selection of liquid refreshment and meals. Ales include Courage, John Smiths, Beamish, Becks and guest beers such as Ruddles and Old Speckled Hen. Outside seating and garden. *Open until 3pm Sat/Sun, closed Monday lunch-time.*

ROM the centre of the village take the lane alongside the small green and telephone kiosk between houses, passing a former pub now converted into a private residence. After about 300 yards, just before the lane sweeps right, go though the first metal gate on your left adjacent to a fence stile and a sycamore tree. Cross the field diagonally cutting off the right corner to a fence stile in the crossing boundary 100 yards ahead, then continue the line forward in the next field to an opening in the opposite boundary between trees.

There are two gateways here – take the left one leading to the left of a hedge which shortly turns to post and wire and winds round the edge of a small hill from where you can see the village of Trefonen in the distance.

The way descends to the end of a field where there is a rickety old stile to cross underneath a holly tree. Continue with a hedge on your right to pass through a gateway and bear slightly right up a rise and onto a path to the right of an oak topped knoll.

At the top of the rise proceed forward with a hedge on your right and Bellan Farm and Treflach Hall below, but only for about 100 yards until reaching a gate. At this point cut half left across and up the same field towards the left of a line of oak trees 100 yards ahead and you will find a rather crude but waymarked stile giving access into the adjoining field. Bear half left, aiming to the left of a belt of trees on the bottom boundary and in the left corner cross a waymarked stile onto a lane. **1**

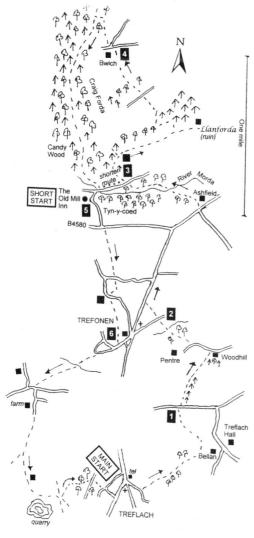

Turn right then left after 20 yards into a field keeping to the right boundary as it descends to a gate at the far end. Don't be tempted to veer off left to a stile which you may be able to see in the left corner. Go through the gate and continue the line forward with the hedge on your right as Woodhill Farm comes into view and the path leads onto a short track alongside a stone wall before exiting onto another lane.

Bear left here, cross a cattle grid after which the surface becomes a little worn and, where it swings left towards Pentre Farm, continue your line forward across a small section of field following the line of telegraph poles (not electricity poles which are further to your right) to reach a small wood. You enter onto a fairly well defined path which dips through the trees to exit into a rough field dotted with gorse bushes.

18

The path loops a little to the left between the gorse to a fence stile and gate in a crossing hedge.

Proceed over the next field directly to a footbridge over a brook and through the ensuing small paddock, on the far side of which is a hedged boundary going away from you towards houses ahead. Both sides of the hedge are walked but the map shows that the less obvious route to the left is the right of way through a weighted metal gate, up the adjacent field and through another gate at the top into a lock-up garage compound. Cross the compound to arrive at a junction with a lane leading from the village of Trefonen (where there is a pub and shops if you need refreshment already!). **2**

Cross the lane and go over a stile into a playing field, following the right hand edge of it to exit via a kissing gate onto a road where you turn right. It is necessary to walk along this road for about three quarters of a mile and, although it can be busy at times, there is a footpath. Opposite the second turning on the right there is a waymarked stile to cross into the grounds of Ashfield Hotel.

Keep to the left hedge to cross a gravel car park onto a tarmac driveway leading away from the building. As this swings left after 100 yards or so continue on it over a cattle grid with the River Morda below on your right. Go over another cattle grid and cross a bridge over the river towards an attractive farmhouse. Immediately in front of it the track loops left to follow a course parallel to the river, which is now on your left.

Go over yet another cattle grid to walk through a pleasant valley before passing through a waymarked gate in front of two cottages. On reaching the second cottage, continue forward across a grassed area and through a wicket gate beside a large shed. Now bear half right up a rather steep embankment moving away from the river, through an arbour of laurel to find at the top a stile exiting onto a lane. **3**

Cross directly onto a broad public footpath leading into a wood. Ignore a fork left after 200 yards and at a T-junction by a small brick/stone barn continue straight on along another broad track towards a cottage. Pass to the left of the cottage and through a timber gate into a field bearing slightly right away from the tree line and to the left of a circle of stones, which was presumably at one time a sheep pen or similar.

You now follow an indistinct path through some pretty parkland parallel with a line of small trees on top of a brow about 150 yards off to the left. The line is not crucial – a fir wood comes into view on your left and there are some buildings below it ahead. You come to a halt at a dry stone wall and should find a timber gate adjacent to a stile. The buildings are in fact the rather spectacular ruins of Llanforda Hall, a huge country residence containing eleven bedrooms, occupied in the eighteenth century by the Williams-Wynn family. In about 1780 it was burnt down and then rebuilt early the following century. Having fallen into ruin it was auctioned for demolition in 1948.

DO NOT CROSS THE STILE. You now have to do one of those occasional seemingly illogical things in order to stick with the definitive route and almost double back on yourself. Turn left alongside the wall which soon becomes a post and wire fence and runs along the lower edge of Llanforda Wood. Ignore a timber gate into the wood and where you reach the end of it cross a stile to turn right along the adjacent side until you reach the end of a field. Here bear left along the top edge of the same field following a mixed tree boundary on the right.

The way climbs quite steadily and, on gaining level ground, there is a stile in a crossing hedge giving access onto a broad track. You cross this more or less directly to negotiate a fence stile into another field. Head towards trees on the opposite side on a bearing slightly right to find a stile in front of them. Cross onto a narrow path into the wood but after only about 15 yards veer left by a waymark post to a footbridge and stile on the far side.

In the next field follow the post and wire boundary on your right for some 100 yards before crossing a fence stile in it and a footbridge beyond. From here bear half left diagonally across a large field towards Bwlch Farm ahead (to the left of a more modern house which you will probably see first). Exit onto a track via a gate in front of the farmhouse, a beautifully mellow stone built property, and turn right to reach a lane after another 100 yards or so. **4**

Turn left onto the lane and after 30 yards, where it swings right, go through a waymarked gate and then another to the left of a barn and into a field. Continue the line forward with a hawthorn tree boundary on your left, rising gently. At the top cross a stile and press on over a further stile with a pretty house in the valley below on your right. After 100 yards the path swings left over a stile into a wood and at a junction with a broader track after 120 yards bear left onto Offa's Dyke Path. Cross a stile to exit from the wood on to a narrower path which descends, then re-enters the wood. Keep to the main path through Graig Forda on the route waymarked with an acorn, the Countryside Commission symbol marking Offa's Dyke Path.

OFFA'S DYKE PATH. _This coast to coast long distance path runs the length of the England-Wales border from Chepstow in the south to Prestatyn in the north. The Dyke itself was built in the late eighth century by Offa, King of Mercia to define a frontier between his kingdom and the various Welsh kingdoms to the west and to control trade. The earth bank was generally about 6 ft high and 60 ft wide and ditched, usually on the west side, although there are variations in construction probably as a result of each landowner along the route having responsibility for work on his own section. Of the 81 miles of earthworks that can be traced today, 60 are contained within one unbroken stretch between Knighton and Chirk and you are on part of that now._

You shortly turn right by a timber gate, immediately after which keep left at a fork to walk along an escarpment overlooking a deep gorge below with super views over the hills beyond. The views are actually better in winter than summer when trees in full leaf tend to obscure it. On reaching another fork bear right with the acorn as the path descends round to the right of a rocky outcrop.

Ignore all turnings off, including one to the right, until you arrive at a junction with a broader track; here you do go right then almost immediately left continuing the descent through the wood. At the base bear left along the lower of two paths, still following the acorn, to emerge into a valley at Tyn-y-coed. Turn left along a driveway in front of a house and on reaching a lane bear right to take a well earned break at the Old Mill Inn. **5**

Having walked about two thirds of the route on a warm summer's day and sat in the very pleasant garden cooling off for some time I found that my legs required major persuasion to work again, particularly as I knew that an uphill section was to follow. You will need to turn right on leaving, along a lane which ascends around the rear of the pub and after a quarter of a mile reaches a junction where you go left then immediately right over a waymarked stile.

This leads into a field where begins the most prominent section of the Dyke on the walk. You can if you wish traverse a path along the top of the Dyke and after crossing the second stile the path drops to the right of it to exit onto a lane via another stile. Again turn left, then immediately right over a further stile to continue on the path following the left field boundary. Farm buildings and the village of Trefonen are off to the half right.

You will reach a stile in a crossing fence but do not cross it; instead bear right along the bottom boundary of the same field, at the end of which is the biggest stile you are ever likely to encounter, made from old railway sleepers. Once over it, cross a small transport yard to a lane which you go straight across through a gate onto a broad farm track. Keep on it as the surface becomes grassy, past some houses and through a wicket gate onto a narrower path between hedgerows to exit onto a tarmac lane. The splendid Victorian 'Old Malthouse' is on the corner which presumably at one time was connected with brewing at the Efel Inn below in the village centre. **6**

Turn right and stay on the lane for about 250 yards until it bears right and here continue ahead along a grassy path between dwellings to cross a stile into a field. Press forward with a holly and mixed tree boundary on your right which shortly turns to hedge. At the end cross a stile by a brook bearing half left over a stone footbridge and proceed in the next field to a further stile 100 yards ahead.

Cross and continue the line forward, rising through an undulating field towards trees ahead and, at the end, cross another stile onto a lane. Bear left then right along a narrower lane towards farm buildings. Keep on it as it swings left in front of the farm to pass through a waymarked gate.

After a while you join another visible section of the Dyke on top of a rocky outcrop and eventually descend for a short distance to a gate and waymark directing you right across a field. Ignore this, for here we depart from Offa's Dyke, and continue ahead through a gate on the same track which now becomes more stony. On coming to a farmhouse on your left continue forward (i.e. do not follow the track around to the property itself) across a scrubby bit of field to join a narrow path heading towards some trees.

Go through a gate and bear left along a waymarked path in front of a huge disused quarry. The quarry ceased to be viable for limestone extraction and was closed in the 1970s, although there are plans to bring it back into profitable use as an 'equestrian playground'. There are magnificent views across it to Moelydd and the hills beyond before the track dips to reach a five-way junction.

Go straight across up steps over a waymarked stile into a field, and keep to the left boundary around to the rear of the barns and bear left at the top left corner through a gate. This leads you onto a track going downhill in a wood. Do not be tempted to stray over to the right towards another group of trees on a small knoll.

After about 75 yards, by an old tree stump and before the track winds left, bear right across a field to a stile which may not be immediately visible 50 yards ahead behind a small mound. Cross this and the track beyond into a field, following the right boundary of hazel trees. At the end cross a stile and bear left onto a broad grassy track. Continue ahead as it joins a stone driveway for about 50 yards to reach a tarmac lane and here keep the same line forward to exit onto a road after a further 50 yards, back into Treflach.

SHORTER WALK

FROM the Old Mill Inn, point 5, go back to the main lane in front of it and turn right. To avoid any confusion I am not referring to the lane which runs immediately in front of the pub. The lane rises and after about a quarter of a mile it levels out at a point where there is a crossing right of way. This is point 3 on the main route and you bear left along a broad public footpath leading into a wood and follow the main route between points 3 and 5 to return to the starting point.

5
Weston, Lee Brockhurst and Stanton

FACT*file*

MAPS: Landranger 126; Pathfinder 848

DISTANCES: 8½ miles; shorter walk 3¼ miles

MAIN START: Alongside the Church in Weston-under-Redcastle which is off the A49 about 11 miles north of Shrewsbury and nine miles south of Whitchurch. GR565288

> **Public Transport:** Very limited bus service 514 from Shrewsbury (Sat only) calling at Weston under Redcastle. *You may prefer to start from Stanton (see below).*

SHORT START (page 28): From The Stanton in Stanton Upon Hine Heath, one mile west from the B5063, two miles north of Shawbury, or take the A53 from Shawbury and turn left after 2½ miles. GR568240.

> **Public Transport:** Bus services X64 from Shrewsbury calling at Stanton.

TERRAIN: Easy going through varying landscape with good views over North Shropshire countryside. One or two climbs but nothing too major. Sandstone features very prevalent along various sections of the walk. Suitable for any time of the year but some cropped fields or overgrown paths cannot be ruled out in the summer.

THE PUB: The Stanton is a friendly village pub with bar, lounge and pool room. Bar snacks and meals usually available. There is a good selection of ales including Drawwell (local brew from Wem), Ruddles, John Smiths, Websters Dark Mild, Beamish, Holsten Lager and Strongbow. Garden seating.
Open Sunday lunch-time only, and every evening from 7 p.m. and 5 p.m. on Sat.
If you are walking on any other day in the summer you may prefer to start from The Stanton to take advantage of evening opening.

WESTON-UNDER-REDCASTLE. A picturesque village and home of the renowned Hawkstone Park which contains a number of follies visible from various points on the walk, as well as caves and mature grounds. It is open to the public and well worth a visit but I would suggest this would be better done on a return trip. The Hall was owned by the Hill Family, wealthy local landowners, who also funded most of the cost of building the Church in 1791. It was used as a prisoner of war camp during the second world war (the Hall that is, not the church). Adjacent is Hawkstone Park Hotel and Golf Club together with the remains of 'Red Castle' which dates from the thirteenth century.

URN left along the lane away from the church and immediately left again along a minor lane signed Lee Brockhurst. You will pass a farmhouse on the left and after a further 250 yards on the brow of a hill bear left down a waymarked path between hedgerows. Continue for about a quarter of a mile before crossing a stile on the right into a pasture field and follow the waymark along the line of electricity poles from where, on a clear day, long distance views can be enjoyed over to the right. After the second pole bear half right to a stile in a crossing fence to the right of a gate and proceed in the next field with a post and wire boundary on your right. It bends to the right, descends gradually and (be a little careful here) as it bends right again by an oak tree continue forward down into a hollow to find a stile 30 yards ahead just in front of trees bordering the A49.

Cross the stile and turn left along the verge to the main road for about 200 yards only through a newish sandstone cutting and cross carefully to turn off right through a gateway into a wooded area. If you are following the O.S. map you may be a little confused at this point and wonder where the sharp left bend has gone before realising that the new cutting has taken it out. After going through the gateway you will actually walk along a section of the old road with its white lining still visible.

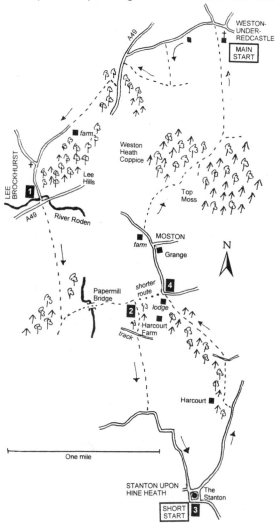

About 100 yards after the gateway, branch left along a sunken track around the edge of a copse which shortly emerges onto a path running between fields. On meeting a junction with a farm track continue forward and forward again when in turn this track meets the driveway up to Lee Hill Farm on the left. The way now becomes metalled and exits onto a lane opposite farm

24

buildings in the hamlet of Lee Brockhurst. Here, turn left and cross a bridge over the River Roden to meet the A49 again but, before doing so, a diversion right is recommended to see the church and other buildings of interest. **1**

LEE BROCKHURST. *A charming farming hamlet mentioned in the Domesday Book and containing a number of buildings of historic importance. To the north (i.e. right at the junction with the lane referred to above) is St. Peters Church, a tiny twelfth century sandstone building with an unusual carved altar head depicting a scene from the last supper. The bridge over the River Roden was built to Thomas*

Bridge over the River Roden at Lee Brockhurst

25

Telford's design in 1800 and, in between, is the small village green from where access is available to the National Trust's protected area of Lee Hills. There is a tableau giving details of the routes through the woods here to a splendid vantage point overlooking the countryside towards Wem. It is a winding path involving a fair bit of climbing and, whilst well worth doing, a return trip would be advisable. As you will have gathered already there is enough to see and do in this area to keep you occupied on another day. Opposite the green are the North Shropshire Hunt kennels and to the east the old forge and school.

Cross the A49 directly up a track running to the left of a dwelling. This track of sandstone bedrock is part of the Shropshire Way and passes through a gate, gradually rises, then levels out to pass to the left of a belt of mixed woodland. As you walk along here there are lovely views to the left over Top Moss and Bury Wood. Ignore a track to the right after going through another gate and continue along the edge of the wood as the path descends on an attractive sunken stretch between sandstone outcrops.

About 150 yards after the end of the wood turn sharp left at a junction and a further 400 yards or so will bring you to Papermill Bridge, where you cross the River Roden again. On gaining a cottage (white painted at the time of research) continue forward along a grassy track to the left of it and negotiate the short ascent of Papermill Bank. As the ground levels out you will pass a converted cottage to meet and continue ahead along a broad driveway. After a further 150 yards or so keep a sharp lookout for a waymarked stile on your right between two oak trees. **2**

Cross the stile and follow the post and wire boundary towards trees just ahead where you will cross another stile to descend through a short section of woodland to a further stile after about 75 yards. Cross this and on meeting a farm track continue forward to the right of a tall buttressed brick wall. After 50 yards the track loops right to a farmhouse but you continue ahead over a stile still with the wall for company. Cross a waymarked fence into a field and follow the left boundary along the edge of a wood and, where the wood ends, continue the line forward across the bottom end of the field to a waymarked stile on the far side of a farm track.

Now, be careful! Cross the stile into a field and bear half left to pass just to the right of two sycamore trees aiming for an isolated beech ahead, just beyond which there is a waymarked stile in the corner of two meeting hedges. In the next (large) field keep on the same line to cross it diagonally towards the right of a group of trees on the opposite boundary. If the field is planted or ploughed up it may be more practical to walk around the edge to the same point. On arriving at the said point exit onto a lane and turn left to follow a zigzag course for half a mile into the village of Stanton Upon Hine Heath. On your right you can see the remains of Moreton-Corbett Castle (open to the public). On reaching a junction continue forward and follow the lane round to find the The Stanton. **3**

Try not to make yourself too much at home – you are still only just over half way round. On leaving, turn left then immediately left again up a lane

The path through Weston Heath Coppice

signed Booley & Moston. In half a mile you will pass the rear entrance to Harcourt and 125 yards or so further on there is a waymarked stone stile and fence in the hedge on your left. Cross, bearing slightly right in the field towards a wood and, on reaching it, turn right along the top edge. You skirt around an old reservoir and continue the line through a metal gate to reach and cross a driveway.

Go through a gate on the other side and proceed in a field to the left of a house and at the far side is a waymarked stile with nice views off to the right over Top Moss. Cross and press forward in the field parallel with and about 50 yards away from a wood on your left aiming towards more trees ahead. On reaching them cross a stile onto a path alongside the trees to another stile 75 yards further on leading into the wood. You now follow a pleasant track through fir trees for some 150 yards to cross another stile, or the remains of one, and continue forward passing beneath three trees to cross a stone stile before descending down steps to exit onto a lane by Moston Lodge. **4**

If you are following the short route you will bear left here, otherwise go straight ahead on a lane passing to the right of a chapel converted into a rather attractive residence bearing the date 1885. You will presently enter the rural settlement of Moston and pass Moston Grange on the right. Ignore a right turn immediately after it to arrive at Moston Farm which bears the somewhat unwelcoming warning sign to would be callers 'Every third traveller is shot, the second has just left'.

Opposite the end of the farm buildings on the right is a footpath sign and a stile to cross before bearing half left to cut off the bottom corner of a field to another stile in the adjacent boundary. Once over this bear 80 degrees right, gradually moving away from the right hand hedged boundary, cutting off the right corner of the field to a further stile which you can see on the opposite boundary with a wood in the background. Cross this and follow post and wire boundary which turns to hedge and leads you to yet another stile in front of the wood.

Now turn right on a broad track running to the left of some houses with Weston Heath Coppice on your left. It will be noted that this is another sandstone rock track and you will continue on it for some time through an attractive area of mixed woodland.

After passing a line of mature beech trees bear left at a fork to ascend yet another sunken path in a sandstone cutting. This is fairly steep but worth the effort as the surrounding woodland is wonderful, especially in the autumn when the colours are changing. At the top of the incline, branch left along a broad stone lane which continues through a sparsely populated residential area with smallholdings.

Ignore all turnings off until you arrive back at the church. This is in fact the Chapel of St. Luke and built of sandstone, what else. The nave and western tower were built in 1791 with the Hill family bearing the bulk of the cost – see note on page 1. It was restored in 1879, the 54th year of the curacy of the Revd. John Hill, brother of the 2nd Viscount Hill and nephew of the more famous General Lord Hill. The family clearly had a major influence on local affairs for many years.

SHORTER WALK

FROM The Stanton at point 3, pick up the main route and follow it through to point 4 at Moston Lodge. Here turn left in front of the converted chapel along a broad track signed 'No Through Road'. After 400 yards or so you will draw level with a wood on the left and in line with the back of it pick up the stile in the hedge between oak trees at point 2. From here follow the main route back to the pub.

6
Bradley

FACT*file*

MAPS: Landranger 127; Pathfinder 871

DISTANCES: 7½ miles; shorter walk 4 miles

MAIN START: In the village of Church Eaton. Tucked away in the countryside to the south-west of Stafford, Church Eaton can be approached via lanes from the A5 direction through Lapley, west from Penkridge or south from Haughton. Parking is a little restricted in the village and the most convenient place is probably in the street at the Royal Oak pub end. GR844174.

> **Public Transport:** Very limited Green Bus service 7 from Penkridge to Church Eaton (Wed only).

SHORT START (page 33): The Red Lion at Bradley about 2½ miles east of Church Eaton. GR879180.

> **Public Transport:** Very limited Green Bus service 7 from Penkridge to Bradley (Wed only).

TERRAIN: Country Villages and pleasant rural landscape. No climbs of note. Many fields cropped during June-August so these months best avoided.

THE PUB: The Red Lion is an attractive period building with two bars, lounge and a restaurant having a good reputation for food. Ales available are M&B, Worthington, Beamish, Carling plus guest beers such as Fredericks Premium and Innkeepers Special Reserve. Bar snacks. Outside seating.
Traditional opening times.

WALK along the main street of Church Eaton with its mixture of ancient and modern buildings and past The Swan pub, sadly now closed, to arrive at a T-junction with St. Editha's Church on the left. If you can spare the time have a look at the church – there are some interesting artefacts and fine stained glass windows. A leaflet is available regarding the history of the church from the twelfth century and the origin of the name St. Editha. Apparently there is a well located nearby, called St. Editha's well, which is supposed to have healing qualities, especially for disorders of the eyes.

Turn left and follow the road around to the right of the church for about a quarter of a mile. You will go over a bridge and shortly after this look for a stile in the hedge on your right. Cross and bear half left diagonally over the field around the rear of a modern farmhouse to cross another stile in the far corner. Bear right onto a farm track, go over a concrete footbridge and through a gate into a field where you follow the boundary with a brook on your left.

Negotiate a stile in a crossing fence and turn 90 degrees right in the adjacent field. After about 200 yards you reach a pool where the boundary kinks right. The right of way continues directly forward for another 100 yards to a stile in the crossing boundary ahead (although crops forced me to go right and around the edge). There is a little footbridge here to cross, then proceed across the next field heading about 20 yards to the left of a line of oak trees.

On gaining the boundary you will discover another footbridge and stile – cross these into the next field with a hedge on your right. At the end of it, bear left and then go through a gap in the hedge after 15 yards to turn right and double back on yourself for the same distance before turning left to pick up the original line. This might sound complicated but it's not really (famous last words?).

Now cross the centre of a field following a line of oak trees with Green Fields Farm off to the right. Skirt to the left of a hollow and pick up the line of oaks again on the other side then, after the last tree, veer half right for 15 yards through a gap in the hedge to turn left onto a lane. After about 40 yards there is a turning right along a farm track with a hedged boundary on the left. **1**

Follow the track through pleasant countryside as it passes another pool on the right and is joined by a hedge on the left. After a third of a mile or so the track swings left but you continue more or less straight ahead along the right side of a hedge towards Shredicote Wood. Enter the wood on a narrow path, which can get boggy, and emerge via a waymarked gate. Continue the line forward in a field following a line of trees and on the opposite side is a gate exiting onto a broad crossing track. Turn left onto it and after going through another gate you will come to a junction with a narrow tarmac lane.

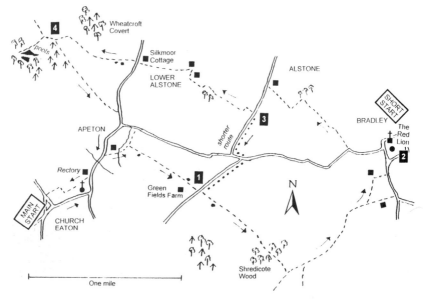

Turn left and walk along the lane through a quiet rural area for about two thirds of a mile to a point some 150 yards before reaching farm buildings where you cross a stile in the hedge on your left into a field. Bear half right across it to the top right corner and cross a stile into another field over which you pass directly to a gate opposite in front of another farm.

Go through the gate and turn right onto a tarmac drive in front of the farm, then bear left on reaching a junction with a lane. Right on this junction is an ancient perpendicular stone known as 'The Webb Stone' and legend has it that, to avoid spinsterhood, local maidens should bow to the stone whenever passing by! Continue on the lane into the village of Bradley and the Red Lion.

> **BRADLEY.** *An agricultural community, the fields around which appear to have kept their ancient boundaries largely intact. There are several coverts and relics of the woodland of the ancient manorial divisions, including Shredicote. The village itself boasts a number of handsome buildings and the Church of St. Mary and All Saints, which has a number of interesting features not the least of which are the outward leaning walls – very similar in this respect to the church at Tugford (see Walk 16).* **2**

On conquering the temptation to linger take the descending lane opposite the pub signed Church Eaton. Ignore a public footpath sign on the left opposite Rose Cottage and continue for a few yards to where the lane bears sharply left. Here cross a fence stile on your right and follow the hedged right boundary of a field to cross another stile at the far end.

The way now becomes a little indistinct for a while. Aim for the hedge corner coming in from the right and, having reached it, strike half left to

Bradley. Approaching the Red Lion

31

cross the centre of a large pasture field aiming a good 50 yards to the left of a lone oak but to the right of a farmhouse further in the distance. You will see a line of oak trees ahead – make towards the left of the line and on arriving at the far field boundary, turn left to follow the top edge of the same field.

After about 150 yards (depending upon the point of your left turn) there is a metal gate directly in line with the farmhouse referred to (Alstone) – go through this and cross the centre of a field towards the buildings and join a line of small hawthorn trees on the left before entering a concrete driveway taking you to the left of the farm to exit onto a lane. Turn left on the lane and after some 300 yards, just before some cottages on your left, branch off right along a rough track. **3**

The track shortly kinks left then right and, although the official line ahead appears to be to the right of the boundary hedge, it is much more sensible to keep on the track to the left of it towards a small copse. The way snakes around the edge of the copse and bears right towards Lower Alstone Farm. Ignore turning right to the farm buildings and continue forward through a small yard area to a gate 40 yards ahead, after which bear right following the field boundary around the rear of the buildings.

A further 150 yards brings you to a gate at the side of a blockwork farm building; go through onto a concrete drive between brick and tile barns which passes to the right of the farmhouse then immediately turns left through a gate onto a narrow lane. This in turn exits after a third of a mile onto a wider lane by Silkmoor Cottage. Cross directly to follow a waymarked path in a field and at the end of it pass a pool on your left and cross a fence.

After a few yards you come to another pool and again the route is to the right of it but you will need to negotiate a metal gate in front of a stile beforehand. Once in the adjacent field proceed with post and wire boundary on your left and Wheatcroft Covert some 200 yards over to the right.

After a while the boundary kinks left then right and although the official route cuts off the corner created by the kink it may be simpler to stick with the field boundary. There is a fir wood in view ahead and the right hand edge of it is our destination, but take care over directions. You will need to look carefully for a lone oak tree and, on reaching it, strike right across the centre of the field towards the left of a line of poplars ahead. You should be closing gradually with the field boundary to your left and walking roughly parallel with Wheatcroft Covert on the right.

At the top left corner to the left of the last poplar is a gate to go through. Your line is now diagonally across the centre of a gooseberry field but unless you are wearing armour plating I would suggest that you bear right along a well defined track around the edge of it with another line of poplar trees on your right to reach the corner of the fir wood. **4**

At the corner of the wood is a junction of paths and our way is left alongside the edge of it. If you wish you can take a short diversion to

Reulemill pools where, on the day of my visit, there were more mallards in one place than I have ever seen before. To do this, turn right and at another junction after 125 yards bear left. At the next junction to the right of a small cottage branch right and the pools, or the one visible one, is immediately on your left.

Back on track, walk along the left edge of the wood and continue on a broad track with the gooseberry field now on your left. Some 200 yards after the wood ends the track loops right but here go through the gap in the hedge on your left then turn right to follow the edge of the gooseberry field again but with the hedge on your right. At the end of the gooseberry field continue forward on a narrow path between trees and after 200 yards meet and go ahead along a farm track.

On reaching a lane bear right past Apeton Manor Farm and into the small agricultural settlement of Apeton. Continue along the lane past Malthouse Farm, Yew Tree Farm and then Bellfields on the left going towards Church Eaton. You will walk again along a short section of lane travelled on the outward route (in the opposite direction I trust) and cross the same bridge over a brook. Just before reaching a left hand bend with the church ahead, there is a detached house on your right which is in fact the Rectory.

Look for and cross a stile at the top of a stepped embankment to the left of the house and then go over another stile into a field walking parallel with the churchyard. After 75 yards cross another stile into the next field now taking a line parallel to the main street and at the end bear right to follow the boundary around for about 50 yards before turning left through a gate. This leads onto a broad grassy track alongside some modern houses and, on reaching a junction with a lane, turn left to meet the main street and return to the starting point.

SHORTER WALK

FROM the Red Lion, point 2, follow the main route to point 3 but instead of turning right along the farm track continue on the lane for about another quarter of a mile to a T-junction. Here bear left and after 200 yards veer sharp right along another lane for around a quarter of a mile to reach point 1 and the farm track on your left. This turn is easy to find on the main walk approaching from the opposite direction but you may need to keep a sharp look out for it. The best I can say is that you should look for an opening in the field boundary on your left at the end of a straight stretch of lane just after it has curved slightly to the left. If you reach the driveway to Green Fields Farm on the right you have gone too far!

From point 1 pick up the main route again back to point 2 and the Red Lion.

7
Melverley

FACT*file*

MAPS: Landranger 126; Pathfinder 868

DISTANCES: 8¼ miles; shorter walk 3¾ miles

MAIN START: In Melverley along the lane between the Tontine Inn and the church. From Shrewsbury, take the A458 Welshpool Road and after about five miles, bear left along the B4393 for another five miles to Crewgreen before turning right over the River Severn to Melverley one mile to the north. GR 333166.

   Public Transport: Nothing suitable to Melverley. However, there are very limited bus services from Oswestry to Crew Green (service 565, Tues and Sat), and to Pentre (service 571, Sat only) which is about a mile from the Royal Hill Inn. You may wish to start your walk from one of these points.

SHORT START (page 38): As above – the short and long routes on this walk both start from The Tontine.

TERRAIN: Riverside, fields and quiet lanes in attractive border country. Absolutely no climbs at all. Some fields may be planted and the occasional path overgrown in summer so either side of June – August may be best.

THE PUBS: The Royal Hill Inn, Edgerley: Quite unique – this pub is like a time warp, not seeming to have moved into the twentieth century. It was built in 1777, or so the date stone tells us, and is a small, fairly isolated riverside local of great charm and a focal point for the surrounding agricultural community. There are two small bars with quarry tile floors, one of which is literally not large enough to swing a cat in and there are no modern trappings at all. Ales on offer include Wadworths 6X, Flowers, Whitbread and Heineken. *No meals. Closed weekday lunch-times.*

The Tontine Inn, Melverley: A rather more traditional establishment and somewhat larger. Although modernised the building is fairly old and maintains its period quaintness. Caffreys, Bass, M&B, Worthington, Guinness and a selection of lagers are available in the comfortable bar/lounge and there is a restaurant area for 'home cooked' meals. Outside seating. *Closed at lunch-times on Mondays and Tuesdays.*

MELVERLEY. *A scattered rural community comprising only 55 houses lying beside the River Vyrnwy but having a long history of over 1000 years. The outstanding feature is St. Peters Church, a stunningly beautiful building and a rare example of early British churches constructed of timber, wattle and daub. It was built in the early fifteenth century of local oak, the entire structure being pegged together without a single nail being used. There are numerous interesting artefacts and relics to see inside, including an unusual gallery made from a huge single piece of oak and an ancient font. A plaque on the churchyard entrance proclaims Melverley to be 'Britain's most motivated village in 1991' – a distinction awarded for raising a quarter of a million pounds to carry out stabilisation works to the river bank, erosion of which was undermining the structure of the church.*

WALK to and though the churchyard and leave by a gate at the far side by Church House onto a public footpath alongside the River Vyrnwy. Cross a stile (the first of many on this walk!) and continue forward along the top of a dyke. This is known as the Argae and, believe it or not, was built as long ago as 1790 by Dutch engineers to contain the flood water of the Severn and Vrynwy Rivers. The Vrynwy actually runs along the Welsh border and on a clear day you can see the mountains of Wales ahead.

Cross two further stiles after which Haim Farm comes into view on the opposite side of the river. Also visible from here and other points on the walk is Rodney's Pillar at the summit of Breidden Hill. It was erected in 1781 to commemorate Admiral Lord Rodney's naval victories over the French but has been the subject of long controversy about why exactly it was sited here as he had no connection at all with the area. One popular theory is that his ships were made of local timber which brought financial benefit to the vicinity. You can also see Criggion very low frequency radio

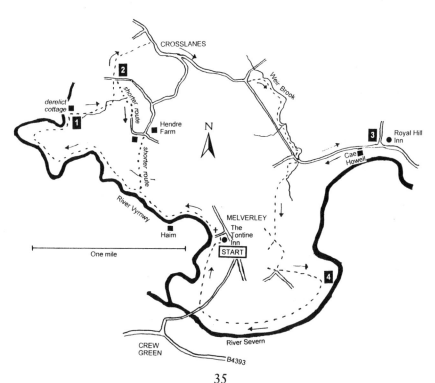

Melverley Church

station which is used for world wide submarine communications. Interesting area isn't it?

After a further a quarter of a mile or so cross a fence stile and continue on the dyke, over a further fence stile and then a double one with a stone driveway between to stay on the dyke. You cross two further stiles after which the dyke swings sharply right and following the next stile it sweeps left towards a derelict cottage. Just before reaching the cottage bear right down the embankment to go over a stile at the base. **1**

Cross the field at right angles to the dyke passing about 20 yards to the left of a lone sycamore to a double stile and footbridge on the opposite hedged boundary. This field can be cropped at times. Once across, bear half right to join the right boundary of a large field and continue with it to the top where you go through a gap in the hedge into the next field.

Now turn almost immediately right by a waymarked fence post through a gap in a hedge into the adjacent field and bear half left to reach another double stile and footbridge about 50 yards ahead. Cross and continue the line forward over the centre of the next field to another stile 150 yards ahead on the opposite boundary. After this is a short section of field to a further stile and footbridge where you exit onto a lane. **2**

Cross the lane directly over another stile and footbridge to follow left field boundary for 50 yards to yet a further stile. Once over continue ahead to a double stile and footbridge in the tree line 150 yards on, cross and then bear slightly right to walk parallel with the left tree boundary to, yes, another double stile and footbridge after a further 150 yards or so. The farm buildings of Crosslanes are now in view and you continue your line

36

straight forward over the next field, cross a stile and follow the right boundary in the adjacent field to exit via another stile onto a lane.

Turn right to pass through the attractive farming community of Crosslanes, ignoring all footpath signs to the right. You will go by a delightful black and white thatched house called 'Foxglove Cottage', shortly after which bear left along a lane signed Pentre. Walk through a scattered residential area and pass a small farmhouse on the right, after which the lane swings left. In another 150 yards there is a broad stone track to the left and you go over the stile to the right of the entrance to it.

Cross the field to the far hedge just to the right of a weeping willow to pick up another section of dyke. Cross a waymarked stile in the hedge into the next field and follow the dyke as it curves right then left with the line of Weir Brook and continue over another stile before crossing a narrow bridge over a sluice. On reaching the next boundary negotiate a double stile to stay on the dyke, followed by three further stiles before rejoining the lane. Before doing so, however, you have to balance on a short narrow beam across another sluice so take extra care here.

Turn left onto the lane and pass Cae Howel Farm on the right after about a third of a mile before arriving at the Royal Hill Inn a short distance further on. **3**

You may notice a waymark opposite across the field to the edge of the River Severn. This path continues on the other side of the river and originates from the days when a ferry operated between the two banks.

When you have decided to depart this unusual hostelry, retrace your steps along the lane to a point just short of your earlier exit onto it and look for a waymarked stile on your left by the road sign for Melverley (which had been removed at the time of my visit). Cross this and the ensuing field directly to another stile on the opposite boundary. Once over turn left onto a broad earth track between trees, which can get a little overgrown in summer, and after 50 yards go over a further stile into rough pasture with Weir Brook again on your left.

You will very shortly spot a derelict brick barn ahead and you bear off to the right of this and go through a gap in the crossing hedge 50 yards further on, ignoring a stile to the right. In the following field follow a course parallel with the hedge, then tree, boundary on your right with the remains of an old road on the other side, to cross a double stile in the bottom boundary.

Continue your line forward in the next field, slicing off the right side of it to the top right corner to exit via a stile which someone has kindly put a gate across! You are now at a crossroads of tracks with a stile to the left and another to the right. Take the former and bear half left over a field to cross a further stile 100 yards ahead in the crossing hedge. Go over the next field and a double stile about 150 yards on in the opposite boundary.

From here it is necessary to bear half right diagonally across a field to what I would say is the top left corner – but I suppose it depends on the angle you are looking from. Anyway I think you will find the way – even if the field is planted there should be a path going across it.

Cross a stile in the corner and turn left onto a track which quickly veers right and go over a stile to the side of a gate in front of you. The distance between the two stiles is only a few yards so don't continue on the track as it turns right. There is now a large field facing you and you bear half right across the centre of it to a footbridge and stile in a group of trees in the distance. Cross and proceed more or less straight forward in the next field until reaching another dyke and turn right onto it. **4**

The dyke follows a course parallel with the River Severn, about 100 yards away from it, and you cross numerous stiles along a distance of around a mile before arriving at a road bridge, which at one time carried a railway over the river. Go under the bridge and bear half right away from the river, then cross a fence stile to enter along the dyke again. Pass through a gate into a field, halfway across which the dyke peters out.

At this point continue forward to meet a hedged boundary in front of farm buildings and turn right to follow the hedge around to a stile in front of a concrete block outbuilding. Cross and turn right onto a stone track leading around the right of this outbuilding to cross a further, and the last, stile to arrive back at the church.

SHORTER WALK

THE short walk also starts from the Tontine as there is not a particularly convenient route around the Royal Hill Inn. Follow the main route through to point 2, the exit point onto a lane. Turn right onto the lane but turn right again almost immediately down a broad grassy track. Ignore a stile to the left after 200 yards or so, following which the track can get overgrown in summer. It eventually becomes metalled on reaching a house and you continue on to pass by a cottage with a crinkly tin roof and barns to reach a junction with Hendre Farmhouse off to the left.

On your right is a stile to negotiate into a large field which you cross diagonally to the far right corner, passing just to the left of a lone oak. At this corner is a waymarked double gateway with stiles – pass through or over into next field and bear half left cutting off the left side to the opposite corner where you cross a footbridge and stile in a dip. Now bear half left across the next field to a stile you can see in the opposite corner about 150 yards ahead. Cross this and climb an embankment to negotiate a stile on the left and retrace your steps along the dyke back to the start.

8

The Shropshire Union Canal
and Belvide Reservoir

FACT*file*

MAPS: Landranger 127; Pathfinder 871 & 891

DISTANCES: 10 miles; shorter walks 3¼ miles, 4¼ miles

MAIN START: In Wharf Lane Brewood, alongside the R.C. church, which is right next to the bridge crossing over the Shropshire Union Canal on the road going out of the village towards Bishops Wood. The Bridge Inn is directly opposite. Brewood is approached via the A5, two miles to the north; from the south via Codsall or westwards from the A449 Wolverhampton – Stafford Road. GR879089.

> **Public Transport:** Green Bus service 2/3 from Wolverhampton, or very limited service 1 from Penkridge, calling at Brewood.

SHORT START (page 43): The Vaughan Arms, Lapley, two miles north of the A5 on the road linking Stretton with Wheaton Aston. GR874129.

> **Public Transport:** Green Bus from Wolverhampton or Penkridge as above calling at Brewood and, less frequently (service 3 from Wolverhampton only), at Lapley.

TERRAIN: Very easy pleasant walking along the canal towpath, across fields and around Belvide Reservoir. Plenty of interest and no climbs. Can be walked at any time although there may be one or two cropped fields during the summer.

THE PUB: The Vaughan Arms is a bit like the 'Tardis' – a lot bigger inside than it looks from the outside. The quaint white painted elevations give way to a modernised yet unspoilt interior with comfortable bars and a superb 'ale menu'. Beers include the whole range of Marstons, Banks's mild, Carlsberg, Red Stripe, Becks, Guinness and Dry Blackthorn and, if that isn't enough to choose from, you can try one of the guest beers.
Normal opening times.

FROM the canal bridge go down the steps to the towpath. Turn right and walk along a straight section of the Shropshire Union Canal for about three quarters of a mile to the first bridge which you can see in the distance. On reaching it climb the embankment up to a lane and turn left over the bridge.

The lane winds through the village of Shutt Green, which is dominated by a mobile home site, and climbs gently to pass a car park on the right reserved for members of West Midlands Bird Club who have private access to the hides on Belvide Reservoir. Continue on the lane for another two

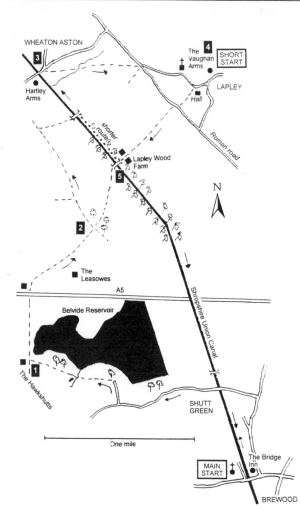

thirds of a mile and look for a broad stony track leading towards some farm buildings. Go along here, passing by the buildings, and after a further 120 yards, opposite the end of a cottage, bear left through the first of many metal gates on this walk and into a field.

Keep to the left and follow a line of oak trees across the centre of the field and, after the last tree, veer very slightly right across the remaining section of field to the next gate in front of a tree line on the far boundary. Go through and over a footbridge, bearing right in a small field at the end of which is the next gate on your left. Now walk with a post and wire boundary to your right, from where you get a good view of the reservoir, and continue on a path around the left edge of Hawkshutts Wood. You pass a sign which advises you that the trees here were planted by the British Trust for Conservation Volunteers in 1993 and after the wood ends continue on towards Hawkshutts Farm ahead. Go through two more gates to exit onto a driveway in front of the walled garden and turn right.

The driveway takes you along the western edge of the reservoir but please do not be tempted to get closer to it by crossing one of the stiles on the right. These are not public rights of way. If you are a 'twitcher' you will no doubt have had the forethought to bring a pair of binoculars to get a closer view of the water birds which abound here. The reservoir is in fact a feeder for the S.U. Canal and was constructed in 1830. It covers a site of 208 acres and is a protected bird sanctuary with restricted access.

Stay on the driveway until it arrives at its junction with the A5, turn left along the main road for about 30 yards, then cross (carefully!) to branch right down a waymarked bridleway to the right of White Gate Farm. Go through a gate onto a track round to the right of the buildings and through another gate into a field. There is a further gate after about 75 yards – which can be a very muddy 75 yards! – taking you into a long field where you continue forward with the boundary on your right. At the end is another gate with The Leasowes Farm off to your right; go through and cross the ensuing open field diagonally to a belt of trees on the opposite boundary where you will find the next gate. You are now at a crossroads of paths with a gate to the left and another to the right. **2**

Take the left gate into a field following a line parallel with the hedged boundary until it kinks left and here continue the line directly forward across the open field aiming to the right of a tree line on the far boundary to find another gate. Just for a change this one is timber. You meet a track curving round in front of the gate and turn right (effectively continuing ahead) onto it. The track is enclosed by hedgerows which in summer tend to obscure the extensive views over surrounding countryside but it nevertheless winds a pleasant way for a little over half a mile into the village of Wheaton Aston. However, you don't stay on it the whole way – just before it loops left towards the village look for a waymark post and kissing gate on your right. The post advises you that you are on 'Monks Walk', the name seemingly derived from the route of an ancient footpath connected with the former Priory situated in Lapley.

Go through into a field and cross diagonally (east) to a stile in the far boundary 150 yards ahead. Having negotiated this, continue the line forward across the next field aiming towards the canal bridge ahead. Before reaching it you cross stiles on each side of a track and one onto the bridge itself. Cross the bridge and bear round to your right onto the towpath and turn right again under the bridge to walk along another short section of 'The Shroppie'.

SHROPSHIRE UNION CANAL. *Engineered by Thomas Telford (who sadly died during its construction in 1834) the 'Shroppie' was the last great narrow boat canal to be built in England. Typified by deep cuttings and high embankments, it took 10 years to complete but never made a profit due to increasing competition from the railways. It was eventually taken over by London North Western Railway and fell into commercial disuse before the end of the last war.*

A distance of around a third of a mile will bring you to bridge 19, with the Hartley Arms on the left. Unless you wish to take a break at the pub, leave the canal and turn right on the lane away from the built-up area. **3**

After a distance of only some 60 yards go over a waymarked stile in the hedge on your right and cross the field diagonally to the opposite corner. Here there is a gap leading onto a short track into the next field with a sports ground on your left. Keep to the right boundary with a brook and cross a footbridge into the adjacent field.

41

The Vaughan Arms

Turn left now to continue the line forward but with the brook on your left and after a short distance look for a stile off to the half right approximately in the centre of the far boundary. Make for this and in the next field continue the line across it diagonally to the top right corner. Here there are two gates and a footbridge to negotiate before exiting onto a lane. Bear right on the lane, which is in fact an old Roman road, and then left after 50 yards along Church Lane towards Lapley. You will pass All Saints Church which, unfortunately, is kept locked but there is a list of keyholders posted by the entrance door for those wishing to look inside. Keep going as the lane swings left by Lapley Hall to arrive at the Vaughan Arms after another 200 yards or so. **4**

LAPLEY & WHEATON ASTON. *Although one parish the two villages are separate communities, lying each side of the route of the Roman road crossed earlier. Lapley is dominated by its twelfth century church, the land for which was given to Benedictine monks by Alfgar, a son of Lady Godiva of Coventry. Up to the eighteenth century Wheaton Aston was regarded as something of a spa due to the existence of mineral waters and a healing well. It is also the most northerly location of a rare flower, Snakes Head Fritillary, which is the unofficial 'emblem' of Wheaton Aston. Sounds like a good question for Mastermind!*

It might require a determined effort to leave this comfortable hostelry but, on doing so, retrace your steps to Lapley Hall where the lane swings right. On the corner, directly opposite a cottage, bear left through a gap into a field and follow the left boundary. At the end you reach a surfaced crossing track by a cottage and turn right onto it for a short distance until reaching a junction with the Roman road again.

There are a few signs around indicating that you are now on the

Staffordshire Way and you cross the road directly down a broad metalled track. After about half a mile you arrive at Lapley Wood Farm and continue ahead on a concrete driveway between the farm buildings. Beyond the buildings is a grassy track between hedgerows which leads you through a gate to a bridge over the canal. **5**

Bear left in front of the bridge down an embankment and turn left again onto the towpath which will take you the remaining 2¾ miles or so back to the starting point. On the way you pass through an area which, in summer at least, has almost tropical characteristics with larger and thicker trees on both sides which in places touch each other over the water. A small marina precedes a crossing of the aqueduct bridge over the A5 built by Thomas Telford in 1832. You can really appreciate the amount of heavy labour that must have been used to construct the high embankments along this section; a world apart from the pretty and peaceful place that now provides recreation for narrowboat enthusiasts. When walking along this path my eyes locked on to one of these boats in the distance which I assumed was coming towards me. After a while it occurred to me that the distance between us was closing extremely slowly; then the penny dropped – we were in fact moving in the same direction but I was walking at a slightly faster rate than the boat! It must be very therapeutic to slow the pace of life down to this level. The A5 bridge is followed after three quarters of a mile or so by two further bridges close together, the second of which is at Shutt Green where you left the canal on the outward route. Now simply reverse the initial stretch to finish.

SHORTER WALK

STARTING from the Vaughan Arms, point 4, follow the main route to the bridge on the Shropshire Union Canal, which is point 5. Here the main route takes the embankment path to the left of the bridge but you should bear right down onto the towpath and continue on it for around three quarters of a mile, exiting at the bridge by the Hartley Arms, point 3. From here, pick up the main route again back to the pub.

As an alternative you could take a slightly longer walk by following the main route to the bridge at point 5 and cross it to pass through a metal gate. After 20 yards turn left onto a concreted track. This shortly loops right towards a gateway but before reaching it branch right to a waymarked metal gate and onto Monks Walk. Follow the right boundary of a field and continue ahead along a narrow path between trees until you reach the crossroads of paths at point 2. There are three gates to choose from – take the one to your right and follow the main route back to the Vaughan Arms.

9
Worthen and Brockton

FACT*file*

MAPS: Landranger 126; Pathfinder 888

DISTANCES: 8¾ miles; shorter walk 4½ miles

MAIN START: In the lane opposite All Saints Church in Worthen where there is ample space in a square. The village is located on the B4386 about 10 miles south-west of its intersection with the Shrewsbury ring road. GR328047.

   Public Transport: Limited bus service 558/561 from Shrewsbury calling at Worthen.

SHORT START (page 49): The Cock Inn, Brockton about three quarters of a mile further along the B4386 towards Montgomery. GR317045.

   Public Transport: As above. The bus service also calls at Brockton.

TERRAIN: Up hill and down dale with some good viewpoints. There are two fairly stiff climbs. In summer some fields may be planted and paths overgrown in places. Spring and autumn are probably the best times for this walk.

THE PUB: The Cock Inn at Brockton is a simple but friendly local with lots of home drawn cartoons of regulars around the walls. Good selection of ales including Burtonwood, Castle Eden, Boddingtons, Labatts, Carlsberg and Guinness. Excellent fresh rolls, cobs and pies available.
Normal opening times.

WORTHEN. *A pretty, predominantly rural village although it does have a long history of a more industrial nature. Worthen Brook, which rises in the hills to the north, was the village's 'power station' and a mill supported corn, timber, wool and cider industries. Indeed, times were once so prosperous that there were six pubs in the village; now, alas, there are none. Nevertheless, there is still a thriving local community based on the village hall. The ancient parish church was founded in Anglo-Saxon times and has a Norman tower with a ring of six bells.*

CROSS the B4386 and enter a public footpath to the right of the church. You are soon joined by a brook on the right and shortly thereafter pass a (small!) sewage works. Keep to the right to cross a footbridge and stile into a field and follow a path parallel with the brook aiming for another stile to the left of a gate on the opposite boundary. Cross this and stay with the mixed tree boundary as it weaves in and out with the line of the brook, but after 120 yards or so take a footbridge and stile on your left into the next field.

Keep to the timber post boundary and in another 200 yards cross the brook again via a further footbridge on the right and follow the right hedged boundary in the next field. A distance of around 150 yards will bring you to yet another footbridge and stile in the hedge which you cross and continue with the hedge on your left. It kinks 90 degrees left after which point you should be able to see an oak tree directly ahead.

About 100 yards before reaching the tree swing half right across the field to a stile 100 yards in front in the opposite boundary to the left of another oak. There is a little footbridge to cross before the stile and afterwards you have a brook for company as you cross a rough pasture field with pleasant views to the right over the area just walked with hills behind which are our eventual destination. Just prior to reaching the field corner, which you can't actually get to, there is a stile on the left leading to a short stepped embankment up to a lane. **1**

Turn right to pass a farm and then left along a lane signed Hope and Bentlawnt. The lane climbs gradually to start with, then continues more steeply past an isolated cottage and almost at the top you reach Blue Barn

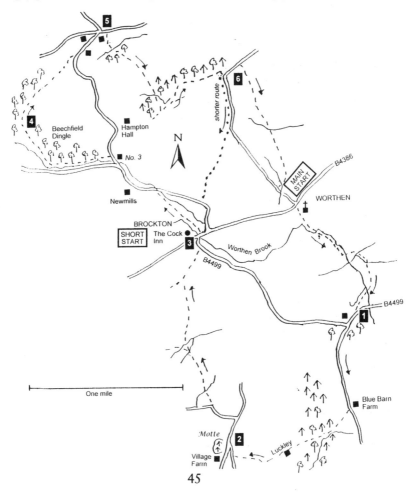

45

Farm, although there were no blue barns in sight at the time of my visit. On the opposite side is a pretty black and white cottage – ignore the stile to the right of it but take the next a few yards further on leading down a stony track. You shortly pass through a waymarked gate onto a grassy (and sometimes muddy) farm track.

After going through another waymarked gate the track loops right across a fairly deep gorge, immediately following which bear half left to cross a stile 40 yards ahead in front of a mixed wood. Ignore the path dropping down to the left and take the rising track in the wood with the gorge below on your left. It climbs steadily to exit via a waymarked gate into a field and here bear very slightly left around the left edge of a small hillock surmounted by oaks. There is a waymark post at the left edge directing you to continue along the base of the hillock and, at the corner, the way carries straight on with views opening up over the hills beyond Brockton.

Go through a gap in a crossing hedge by an ash tree and continue your line forward to meet a broad farm track. Bear left along it passing to the right of Luckley Barn, through a metal gate and then turn right to find two more metal gates. Take the right hand one over a waymarked stile alongside it and onto a grassy track following a hedge on your right.

At the field corner there is a stile to the right of another ash tree – cross and bear half right to a further stile 30 yards ahead, clipping off the bottom right corner of the field. You are now starting a descent through rough pasture bearing half left towards Village Farm with its small white painted cottage to the front. Negotiate a stile in a crossing hedge and continue your line forward, still aiming for the farm and, directly in front of it, you are funnelled into a track between hedgerows and through a metal gate. Swing immediately right to follow the waymark along a track to the right of the buildings to exit onto a lane. **2**

Turn right (spot the Motte behind the farmhouse with conifer trees dotted on it) and walk along the lane as it descends past an exquisite black and white timber cottage and what at first looks like a school opposite bearing the date 1872. Closer inspection will reveal that the building has been converted to residences. Branch left at a fork along a lane signed Betton and Lower Wood continuing for maybe 300 yards to where it swings sharply left.

Ignore the first footpath sign on the right but take the second about 15 yards further on almost on the crown of the bend. You have to scramble up a little embankment to get to a stile but, once in the field, cross diagonally to a stile which you can probably see in the opposite corner. There is also a footbridge here to cross before entering a long field following a course along the right boundary, aiming for the top right corner. Here cross another footbridge, ignoring a stile on the left, to proceed on a path through a small spinney. There is yet another footbridge after 25 yards leading into a field where you bear slightly right to a stile 150 yards or so ahead in a crossing fence.

The right of way is now directly forward, cutting off the bottom left corner of the next field (but I found it easier to walk alongside the left boundary because of crops). At the end of the field go through a metal gate onto a farm track between hedgerows. This loops left to reach a T-junction and here turn right to follow the track for about a quarter of a mile until it exits onto the B4499. Turn left and then right on meeting the B4386 after 100 yards to find the Cock Inn on the left in the village of Brockton. **3**

Slipping into a state of lethargy would not be wise – there is some climbing to do yet! Leave the pub turning left and after literally 15 yards follow a waymark left along a partially surfaced access road to farm buildings. Go through a waymarked gate towards the buildings (don't take the path left through a metal gate) and pass to the left of a corrugated metal barn into a sort of farmyard area. On the other side is a waymark post directing you straight across the centre of a large field.

Now, if this field is planted and you find the prospect of crossing it rather daunting, your only option is to return to the main road, turn left then left again up a lane for about half a mile and you will reach the stile referred to at the end of this paragraph. Otherwise, the course is parallel with a brook on your left for a while, but as that loops around to the left continue forward on the same line to the right of a line of oaks to reach the far right corner of the field where you meet another brook on your right. Follow the brook through the next field until exiting onto a lane via a stile on your right.

Turn left (or continue on if you have taken the lane option) up a gentle incline past the attractive Newmills Cottage, after which the lane drops down to a fork. Go to the right over a ford, past another cottage called Arcadia and then a small bungalow simply numbered '3'. You can, if you wish, continue now on the lane all the way up to point 5, and indeed in mid summer it may be better to do so as the alternative off lane route can get overgrown in places.

After a further 30 yards turn left with a waymark in the hedge and drop down to cross a plank footbridge. Immediately cross a farm track and go through a waymarked gate in the fence opposite and into Beechfield Dingle. Press forward with Brockton Brook on your left and a steep bank on the right. This path can become overgrown but eventually it curves right and rises above the level of the brook and, at this point, you will see a derelict cottage ahead. Go to the right of it over a waymarked stile and proceed along a track to join a grassy lane. In about 300 yards alongside a Shell petrol pump (last offering fuel at 6/3d a gallon including tax!) there is a metal gate and two waymarks. **4**

Take the way along the higher track up though a gate and climb towards an angular prefabricated bungalow. You curve sharply round to the right in front of it to reach a metal gate and waymark in the left corner. Go through and climb up a grassy bank keeping to a hedge on your right and, about 30 yards after it turns sharply right, bear left to go between two rows of sparsely spaced trees.

Follow a track forward, rising gently with brilliant views to your left, through a lightly wooded section keeping up to the right and out into an open grassy area. Follow the woodland boundary now on your left until you find a post and wire fence in front of you. Just down to the left you will see a waymarked fence stile – cross to turn right onto a farm track and after 15 yards bear left through a waymarked metal gate into a large field with a rounded hill in front and having a fenced Christmas tree plantation on top.

Aim for the top of an oak tree just visible to the right of the hill and as you rise you will see a waymarked stile about 10 yards to the left of it. Cross and bear right following the hedge on your right. A second hedge begins to the left and at this point there is a stile in the hedge on the right. DO NOT CROSS but go ahead into another field and follow the left hedge up the hill until it turns sharply left and here bear slightly right to the top right corner of the field where you will cross a stile. There is a small boggy area to negotiate before turning right over a culvert bridge and continuing forward for about 30 yards to a metal gate with a stile to the right. Once over this turn left up a lane past a farm to arrive at a crossroads by a quaint little former church now converted into a beautiful private residence. From here it's mainly downhill, I promise. **5**

Turn right and after 20 yards right again along a waymarked path alongside farm buildings to a stile on the other side of the farmyard. Cross into a descending field bearing slightly left towards a copse in the valley below and, in front of the trees there is a footbridge and stile to negotiate. The stile is newish but the footbridge is rather past its sell by date so take care. Why they could not have replaced the footbridge at the same time I don't know!

In the wood bear left to keep the brook on your left and you will reach a stile on the far side. Cross and bear slightly left to the top of a rise (I did say *mainly* downhill) and onward to the far left corner of the field, to the right of which is a waymarked stile. In the next field follow a post and wire fence to your left on a descending course, cross a stile at the end and bear slightly right to continue your descent towards a belt of trees aiming for the bottom left corner where there is a waymarked gate. Go through this and over a little brook, then follow the right boundary of the ensuing field until exiting onto a track via a timber gate.

Turn left here and after a few yards there is a stile in the hedge on your left on the far side of a ditch. To avoid crossing the ditch carry on a few more yards and turn left through a gate into a field (the same field you have just come out of!) and bear half right across it to a stile in the corner in front of a wood. If you had turned left after crossing the little brook and along the top edge of the field you would have reached the same point a lot quicker but that is not the official right of way.

Cross the stile and follow the edge of the wood but, just before the end of it look for a stile on your left. If you reach the end of the wood you have gone too far!

Cross and continue on the same course but on the wood side of the boundary fence, pass through a waymarked gate and continue ahead with post and wire fence on your right. After another 150 yards go through a waymarked wicket gate on the right across grass to meet a lane. **6**

Turn left on the lane parallel with the same fence and after 200 yards there is a waymarked stile on the right. Don't go over it as it just enters an enclosed bit of rough but go through the adjacent gate instead and walk down-field with the boundary on your right. At the bottom of the field is another stile which is barbed off, so go through the gate on your right into the adjacent field. After about 100 yards pass through a wicket gate on the left and continue in the next field following mixed trees and a ditch on the right. This wiggles around a bit and can be a little boggy.

A few yards to the left of the bottom corner between trees go through a waymarked wicket gate bearing slightly left across a field aiming for the tree line ahead and in the dip below. Here there is a footbridge to cross and then a stile on the left after 20 yards leading into a field. Climb gradually with a hedge and tree boundary on the right which kinks and then descends with views over Worthen.

At the bottom is a waymarked stile which you cross to continue your line forward in the next field but now with the hedge on your left. At the bottom of this field is a waymarked stile (with a fence in front of it!); cross and bear half right over the field towards the start of a line of electricity poles on the other side just in front of a stone built cottage. There is a gap to the right of the cottage down to a waymarked stile and footbridge exiting onto a lane. Turn left on the lane back to the starting point.

SHORTER WALK

FROM the Cock Inn, point 3, follow the main route through to point 6 and the lane. The main route turns left here but you should continue forward on the lane downhill. The concrete surface turns to tarmac and after about a third of a mile passes dilapidated barns on the left. Just after the lane swings left there is a waymarked stile off to the right. This is in fact a double stile with a few yards between them and leads up into a field where you bear half right to find another stile in the mid point of the opposite boundary under an oak tree.

Cross this and continue your line more or less straight forward over the next field to another stile close to the bottom right corner. In the next field cut off the very tip of the left corner to a further stile in the adjacent boundary 20 yards ahead. Cross and turn right with a post and wire and oak tree boundary on the right to begin with, then gradually edge away from it to find a stile in the top left corner of this narrow field. After negotiating this bear left onto a broad grassy track which descends and becomes semi metalled to pass between dwellings and exit onto a tarmac lane. Turn left and walk the remaining section back into Brockton.

10
Earls Hill

FACT*file*

MAPS: Landranger 126 Pathfinder 889

DISTANCES: 8¼ miles; shorter walks 3¾, 3¼ miles

MAIN START: The village of Longden about six miles south-west of Shrewsbury, probably best approached via the A488 from Hanwood, unless you know your way around the lanes. Limited street or verge parking. GR442064.

NOTE: As the *en route* pub at Habberley is open at lunch-time only on a Sunday, if walking on any other day you may wish to consider starting from Habberley and breaking at the Tankerville Arms in Longden, which has more traditional opening times. Habberley is located two miles to the south of Pontesbury off the A488. GR 398036.

Public Transport: see below.

SHORT START (page 55): There are short walks from Habberley or Longden, depending on your preference. See also note above regarding pub opening times.

Public Transport: Bus services 546/547 from Shrewsbury calling at Longden. Limited service 551 from Bishops Castle (Tues only) to Habberley.

TERRAIN: Forest, hillside and farmland with magnificent views over the South Shropshire hills. Includes the scenic area of Earls Hill Nature Reserve. Some climbs, but well worth the effort. If considering one of the shorter routes, the Habberley alternative involves much more climbing but the views are better. Please note that some of the paths can get very muddy in wet weather or overgrown in summer but should be walkable at any time of the year.

THE PUBS: The Mytton Arms, Habberley is a very cosy and friendly local with a small bar and lounge. Beers include M & B, Worthington and Guinness. Cheese and onion and biscuits on the bar but no meals served.
Open evenings and Sunday lunch-time only.

The Tankerville Arms, Longden – a comfortable, friendly pub with bar, lounge and restaurant. Period atmosphere with beamed ceilings, fireplace etc. A wide selection of ales on offer – Theakstons, Old Speckled Hen, Ansells, Calders, Tetley, Carlsberg, Guinness, plus Scrumpy Jack and Blackthorn Cider. Bar snacks and meals; garden seating.
Normal opening times but closed Mon lunchtimes. Evenings from 6.30 p.m.

LONGDEN. An ancient village mentioned in the Domesday Book and having one of the oldest parish registers in England, dating from 1538. A curious fact is that in the Manor of Longden property descended by what is called 'Borough English' which means that the youngest son and not the eldest inherited, and if there were no sons then the youngest daughter inherited. The origin of this rare custom is uncertain. A tragic event occurred in 1811 when the Pontesford Brook which flows nearby rose suddenly sweeping away all before it and drowning eight people.

FROM Longden village go up Manor Lane to the left of St. Ruthens Church (enclosed by trees and buildings with only the Lych Gate immediately visible) and through a small modern housing development. Where the houses end it contracts to a single width lane which eventually leads to Longden Manor, but after a further 300 yards look for a public footpath sign on your right.

Take this along a broad earth track which turns to grass to follow the

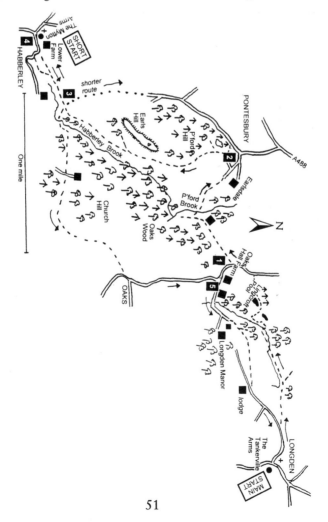

left edge of a small copse, at the end of which is a waymarked stile presenting you with a choice of routes. Our way is straight ahead along a field edge bordering a brook, over a crossing fence and through a double waymarked gate to the right of a small pool, then keeping to the field edge to the left of a belt of trees with the brook now on your right. Another wood will shortly appear on the left, after which look for a waymarked gate on your right; go through and cross the brook again before negotiating a stile a few yards ahead.

Continue forward for 50 yards to reach a small pool. *I cheated here by going along a path to the right of the pool but although this is obviously used it is not an official right of way.* The correct route is left, in front of the pool, on a path which winds through gorse alongside the continuation of the boundary that you were previously following but on the opposite side of it. You will shortly see a footbridge and stile on your left leading into the wood, but do not cross it! Instead bear 90 degrees right following gorse across a field and through a gap in the opposite boundary, after which you will arrive at the far end of the pool.

Turn left by the pool (*I just continued ahead*) to reach a gate into a wood and walk on a path as it passes Lingcroft Pool to exit via timber gates into a field. Follow the left boundary, with good views of the Welsh border hills ahead, to pass through a wicket gate onto a lane in front of some elevated houses with their high retaining walls and follow it as it starts to climb. At the top of the first rise turn right along a broad waymarked bridleway. **1**

The track descends past some cottages to arrive at a gate in front of some farm buildings. Take the narrow path off to the left, continuing the descent through attractive woodland with Pontesford Brook below on the right. At the bottom where the ground levels out into a small spinney there is a waymark directing you right on a narrow path and over a footbridge across the brook.

Cross a little fence stile and climb on a rough path to meet and follow a post and wire fence on the right; cross a second fence stile into an area of sparse trees and continue the ascent to the woodland edge. Here you enter a field and continue your line more or less straight forward to a waymark 50 yards ahead under an oak tree.

Follow the direction along the right boundary of the next field to cross another fence stile and keep ahead to reach a waymarked gate. Go through this and press forward across a boundary fence to pass by the interesting looking Earlsdale Farm before negotiating another fence stile to the right of a timber gate and onto a driveway. Ignore the turning left after 75 yards to meet and continue forward on a tarmac drive which exits onto a lane. Turn left and follow the lane as it ascends for a little over 100 yards and, just before reaching the top of the rise, branch left up a broad track in front of the Forestry Commission sign for Pontesford Hill. **2**

The track loops right after which bear left at a fork along the lower of the two paths following the waymark in the hedgerow. You continue now around the base of Pontesford Hill twisting and turning, rising and falling (rising more than falling I'm afraid!) through pleasant woodland with good views all around. Pontesford Hill is the centre one of three interconnected earthworks along a ridge with evidence of Roman lead mines.

Eventually the way levels out where scenic views open up over Oaks Wood on the left. Ignore all tracks off and continue on the main one signed Shropshire Wildlife Trust. You will go through a waymarked gate into a field and pass a sign to S.W.T. Earls Hill Barn on the left, which houses an exhibition of flora and fauna in the area. If it is open you may wish to visit; otherwise or afterwards continue onward through a gate into Earls Hill Nature Reserve. There is a plaque informing that this is a classified site of special scientific interest because of the variety of habitats present but I will not take up space by going into detail as you can read it for yourselves.

The path becomes narrow and rocky in parts as it winds around the base of the hill and, on reaching more level ground, you come to a waymark post. The main track continues on around the southern end of the hill but you need to turn left down a short embankment and through a gate into a field. Cross the field directly as it leads towards a valley which looks like a huge amphitheatre surrounded by hills. The peak of Lawn Hill is in sight with Broom Hill off to the left.

Go through a gap in a crossing boundary and continue ahead along the right edge of a large field parallel with a wood and a brook on the left. At the top corner you are funnelled into a waymarked track running to the right of a wood and go through a metal gate to proceed with a hedge on your right and an embankment down to the left. After another 200 yards there is a gap in the hedge with a gateway into a field. *Look for and make a note of the waymark post at this point as you will need to pick it up on the inward route.* **3**

In the meantime continue forward on the track, which can get extremely mucky and leads to Lower Farm, beyond which you turn right at a lane into the village of Habberley. However, if you would prefer to avoid the very farmy farmyard take a left turn over a stile about 120 yards after passing through another metal gate. Bear immediately right through a timber gate and follow an elevated path to the right of a post and wire fence. Cross a stile and bear half right over a pasture field to the right of a bungalow in view to cross a further stile alongside it, then another before turning right onto a lane. Follow this into Habberley to find the Mytton Arms on your right. **4**

If you have not sunk into a state of total inertia and you have time, visit the parish church of St. Mary. This small stone building was largely rebuilt during the latter part of the last century although some of the earlier doors and windows remain. There is some interesting stained glass depicting well known biblical subjects connected with the Virgin Mary. Leave the village by retracing your steps to the waymark post at point 3, where those on the short route will turn left towards the west side of Earls Hill. If on the main walk bear right to descend through an area of sparse woodland to cross a footbridge over Habberley Brook.

On the other side follow a waymark half left on a narrow path through trees bordering the brook. After about 60 yards the path leaves the brook to climb a short steep embankment to a stile. Cross and continue the line more or less straight forward across a scrubby field, over a stone farm track still continuing the same line across the bottom corner of the opposite field to reach a stile 100 yards ahead in a crossing boundary beneath some trees. No need to cross it as there is a big gap to the left and in the next field follow the same line diagonally across, climbing steadily to a stile which you may be able to see about 150 yards ahead in front of a wood (don't be tempted to veer off to the left through an inviting metal gate onto a broader track).

Cross the stile and driveway to 'Old Lodge' to climb a short embankment through a waymarked gap into the wood. The path is quite steep and, just before reaching the top, there is a waymarked gate on your right. Go through this and turn left to follow a post and wire boundary. After a while the fence ends and there is another waymark post directing you forward across a further section of the same field.

You are now walking along the base of Church Hill with its small copse on top – the line is not critical although you should be gradually closing with the tree lined field boundary coming in from the right. Before you do close with it you pass through a waymarked gate in a crossing boundary leading onto a track. Go through another gate onto a farm track with superb views on the right over Caer Caradoc and The Lawley and continue until exiting onto a metalled lane by some cottages. Go forward on the lane into the settlement of Oaks. Ignore a turning to the right and stay on the lane for about half a mile until reaching Oaks Hall Farm. **5**

We were amused to see a sign here advertising 'Moo Poo' for sale but declined to take advantage of the offer on the grounds that we had nothing to carry it in! Turn sharp right down the driveway between the farm buildings and cottages (by a post box) and through a timber gate to continue on the tarmac as it loops to the left and passes two further cottages on the left and right respectively.

You now have a wood on your left and, at a fork, bear left to reach some extensive brick buildings which may at some time have been a stable block for Longden Manor. The lane turns to gravel and passes to the left of these buildings and just beyond there is a choice of routes – left down into the wood or straight on through a metal gate into a field. Take the latter and follow the edge of the tree line, passing through another gate, until you reach the end of it. From here continue the line more or less straight forward across the field aiming for Longden Lodge which you can see some of on the far side. The amount of it visible will depend upon how tall you are but, just before reaching it, cross over a fence stile and turn left onto the driveway.

Keep to the left at a fork and after a while you will pass the public footpath on your left entered on the outward route. Now simply follow the lane back to Longden and the start point.

SHORTER WALKS

1. EARLS HILL CIRCULAR – 3¾ MILES

STARTING from the Mytton Arms in Habberley, point 4, turn left through the village past Lower Farm on the left and, where the buildings end, bear left over a stile to the left of a bungalow. Cross another stile into a pasture field and branch half left to a further stile, cross and follow an elevated path around the edge of a field with a post and wire fence on your right. Go through a timber gate and turn immediately left to cross a stile and then bear right onto a wide farm track.

Pass through a metal gate after about 120 yards and continue forward until reaching the waymark post at point 3 with Earls Hill looming large on the left hand side. Turn left here into a field following the left hedged boundary and, after 200 yards or so, pass through a metal gate to proceed with a hedge on your right on a path around the base of a tree covered hillock, which is like a foothill to Earls Hill.

The hedge gives way to post and wire and the path takes you around the base of Earls Hill itself. Go through a waymarked gate and ignore the track uphill on the right to walk along a pleasant path through fringe woodland until reaching a T-junction after about a quarter of a mile. Continue directly forward along a broad stony track which passes by some isolated cottages and then becomes metalled as it descends towards Pontesbury. However, don't continue into the village but turn right at the first junction up a narrow gently climbing lane around Pontesford Hill.

You pass more cottages with views over Pontesbury and the Border hills beyond. Ignore a public footpath sign on the right as the lane starts to descend and continue as it levels out and curves around the hill to pass a couple of further neat stone cottages, the second of which is called Spring Cottage. After a further 50 yards bear right along a waymarked path behind the Forestry Commission sign for Pontesford Hill and join a broad track at point 2. From here follow the main route back to point 3 and through to point 4, effectively reversing the initial section between these two points.

2. LONGDEN – 3¼ MILES

From the Tankerville Arms follow the main route to point 1 but continue on the lane past the broad waymarked track referred to for about 200 yards to arrive at Oaks Hall Farm, point 5. Now turn left down the driveway and follow the main route back to the starting point.

FACT*file*

MAPS: Landranger 137; Pathfinder 910

DISTANCES: 7½ miles; shorter walk 4 miles

MAIN START: In order to construct a walk with the pub conveniently located *en route* I tried to find a parking space along the B4371 between Easthope and Longville on Wenlock Edge. This was not easy – there is a distinct lack of such places. However, there is a lay-by close to Lutwyche Hall at the turn off up Pilgrim Lane which will accommodate 2/3 cars but PLEASE do not obstruct the gateway. GR553945

> **Public Transport:** Very limited. Bus services 170/772 from Much Wenlock, 538/772 from Bridgnorth (Tues, Thurs only), and 540 from Shrewsbury (Sat only) call at Longville.

SHORT START (page 60): The Feathers at Brockton on the B4378 Much Wenlock – Craven Arms Road. GR578938

> **Public Transport:** Very limited bus service 156 from Ludlow (Sat only) calls at Brockton, The Feathers turn.

TERRAIN: Quite easy, passing through open countryside and woodland with a number of interesting features. Gradients of any note are reserved for the second part of the walk but these should not prove too taxing apart perhaps from the one at the very end (sorry about that!). Should be walkable any time of year but some paths can be overgrown in summer.

THE PUB: A real gem! The Feathers has got virtually everything ; olde-worlde charm, antique furniture and fittings, timber beams and large open fireplace. The food menu is truly mouth-watering and earned a place in Egon Ronay Guide 1993-4 . Real Ale is on offer plus Marstons and Banks's – not that the latter aren't real ales but you know what I mean.
Lunch-time opening on Sats & Suns only.
If you are walking during the week in summer you may wish to start at The Feathers to take advantage of early evening opening from 6.30 p.m. (except Mons).

ROM the parking spot walk up Pilgrim Lane until it turns sharp left and here bear right to enter a waymarked bridleway running along the top of the tree line on Wenlock Edge. This limestone ridge runs for 15 miles between Much Wenlock and Craven Arms and was formed in a tropical sea a mere 420 million years ago. The stone has been used for many buildings in the area, including Wilderhope Manor, and is still quarried today for roadstone.

Keep going through four gates ignoring stiles on the right and you pass a old water reservoir with a weather vane on top. There are good views to the left and a stunning vista to the right over Apedale towards the Church Stretton hills although, unfortunately, in summer this is partly obscured by trees in leaf.

You may by now have noticed a marker telling you that this is the Jack Mytton Way. He was an eccentric Shropshire character who lived in the early part of the last century and known as 'Mad Jack'. Renowned for practical jokes he turned to drink and got into debt, was put in debtors prison and died penniless in his late thirties.

Press forward through two more gates to meet a crossing track which kinks left then right to continue on your line. A word of warning here, if not already too late – this path can get rather muddy in wet weather. The way winds gently down to meet a lane by the entrance toWilderhope Manor. Turn immediately left along the driveway to reach it. **1**

WILDERHOPE MANOR. *A limestone manor house dating from 1586 now owned by the National Trust and used as a Youth Hostel. One of its former occupants, Major Smallman, was a Royalist officer in the Civil War and was obliged to flee on horseback from the Parliamentary forces. On reaching a sheer drop on Wenlock Edge with the enemy in close pursuit he made a death defying leap off the edge*

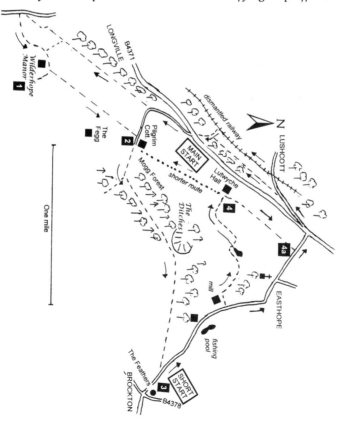

and, although his horse was killed, the Major made good his escape. The house is largely unaltered and features include remarkable wooden spiral stairs, a unique bow rack and fine plaster ceilings. Limited opening Wednesdays and Saturdays 2-4 p.m. April to September, Saturdays only October to March.

Having soaked up the architecture and the history, take a track round the rear of the Manor and turn left onto the Staffordshire Way, proceeding with a hedge on the right. You now follow a course parallel with the earlier route over a stile, through a gate and past the entrance drive to 'The Fegg' to reach a junction with Pilgrim Cottage on your right. It is said that Pilgrim Cottage is so named after some former occupants who sailed on the *Mayflower* to pursue their religious beliefs. Assuming that you will not be moved to do likewise, turn right to pass in front of the house on to a broad track. **2**

You will soon reach some pine trees on the right and after about another 120 yards branch left at a fork and then almost immediately right along a narrower path into Mogg Forest. After climbing gently the path levels out and eventually joins a broad track coming in from the left, shortly after which a derelict farmhouse will come into view in the open field on your right. When almost level with it leave the track to cross a stile in the wood boundary and turn left alongside the edge of the trees along a path which rises then flattens out to skirt to the right of an ancient hill fort known as 'The Ditches'.

Enjoy the expansive views over the Clees to the right but take a little care over direction at this point. About half way round the curve of the fort the path will continue forward and away from it to cross a large field diagonally towards a clump of trees in the distance. In the growing season the considerate farmer marks the path by spraying weed killer but such assistance may not be available at other times! On gaining the right hand corner of the trees you will pass through a gate and the official right of way then continues more or less directly forward to follow a line of electricity poles running parallel with the field boundary. *I found it more practical to follow the boundary itself for about a quarter of a mile to a point where the hedge line juts in towards the poles.*

At the end of 'the jut' there is a fence stile on the left to cross into a pasture field overlooking the valley below. Turn immediately right to enter a broad track which gradually descends towards the road. There is a short downward embankment to negotiate before emerging at a gateway at the side of Ivy Cottage. Go through this and turn right to walk along a lane for a quarter of a mile to The Feathers. **3**

When you can tear yourself away, leave the pub and retrace your steps past Ivy Cottage and continue up this pleasant lane to pass Brockton Grange with an attractively set private fishing pool on the right. The next building on your left is Easthope Mill, a Victorian looking farmhouse which appears as though it has hardly changed since that period. Here you have a choice – tarmac or fields. The tarmac is undeniably pleasant to walk along and takes you through the archetypal Shropshire village of Easthope (see below) to connect with the longer field route at point 4a. If you prefer the fields, turn left down the waymarked drive towards the mill, cross a footbridge and pass to the right of the house.

There is a gate here after which you turn right around the rear of the farm buildings and through a further gate towards the wood in view. Do not go into the wood! Instead, turn half left to a stile in the hedge at the left corner of the wood, cross it into a field and follow the edge until you come to a pool on your right. A peaceful, pretty spot to stop awhile to observe the waterfowl and other wildlife around. At the far edge of the pool cross a stile and then another immediately to the right of it, go over a footbridge and another stile to turn due left following waymark.

Continue with a hedge and a brook on your left with Lutwyche Hall now imposing itself on your right. The Hall is Elizabethan, although built on the foundations of an older building, and commands wide views over the adjacent countryside. A fire in 1989 destroyed the roof and, tragically, the restoration work painstakingly carried out during the previous few years. Formerly a school it is now back in private hands. Again a little directional care is called for here – where the hedge ends turn right across the field passing a small pool to find a stile between barns ahead to the right of the hall. **4**

Do not cross the stile but turn right across the front of the barns on a permissive path parallel to the driveway. Now, with your back to the Hall and with a fence line on your left, you will reach a gate and bear slightly right here to a stile in the bottom corner of the field in front of a house. Cross and go forward on a broad track between hedgerows until you reach the lane at point 4a. Here your way is left up a fairly steep incline to meet the B4371 but, if you have the energy, I would recommend you to take a little diversion into Easthope. The church alone is well worth a visit.

EASTHOPE. *A predominantly farming village with a number of attractive buildings. The only industry recorded here is brick making; baked in a kiln in the field from which the clay was dug and used to build some of the local houses. The Malthouse is medieval and a rare example of cross-wing construction, built with Easthope bricks. St. Peters church was built in the thirteenth century on the site of a Druid worshipping place. It burnt down in 1928 although some of the walls and ancient windows were left intact. In 1333 a previous incumbent Will Germston murdered a patron of the church John Esthope who is supposed to have haunted the churchyard ever since. In the churchyard lie the tombs of two monks from Wenlock Abbey marked with raised crosses. They killed each other at the Manor House after a drunken fight. This peaceful community clearly has a sinister past!*

Cross the B4371 directly, swinging left along and down a lane signed Lushcott and follow it for about a quarter of a mile until reaching a waymark into the wood on your left. Here there is a further choice of routes; one will take you along a dismantled railway line, the other goes into the wood and can be rather boggy in wet weather. Whichever way is chosen you need to look out for your route back to the car. On both routes there is a rather steep climb to finish with so take it easy and you won't need resuscitating when you reach the top.

For the railway route now continue reading from ✷ below.

Taking the higher woodland route enter the track winding its way through the wood and continue on for half a mile ignoring all tracks off including a broad one to the right with fir trees alongside. After this the track dips then rises and after about 200 yards, at the top of a slight incline, you will reach a crossing track – a broad one to the right with a small group of trees and a waymark post on opposite sides of it and a narrower one to the left uphill. Turn left uphill until reaching a stile to the B4371 and the starting point.

✷ Continue on the lane until reaching a bridge crossing. A little scramble up an embankment on the right is required before turning left along the dismantled railway line(which you may be interested to know was a branch of the GWR network opened in 1864 to carry limestone from local quarries to the iron works at Coalbrookdale). Follow it for about half a mile past Lushcott Farm below, ignoring all crossing tracks until you come to a more thickly planted area of fir trees on the left. Between groups of fir trees look for a waymark and a small bridge crossing with a metal rail around it. Here turn left up a broad track (can get overgrown) and over a crossing track to continue climbing uphill to reach the stile onto the B4371 and the starting point.

SHORTER WALK

STARTING from The Feathers, point 3, follow the main route to the stile at point 4. Cross and turn left to pass in front of Lutwyche Hall to walk along a broad straight track for three quarters of a mile passing through three gates to exit at Pilgrim Cottage, point 2 . Turn left here and pick up the main route again through Mogg Forest and back to the pub.

The Feathers, Brockton

12
Worfield

FACT*file*

MAPS: Landranger 138; Pathfinder 911

DISTANCES: 7 miles; shorter walk 2¾ miles

MAIN START: At Severn Park (pay and display) on the A442 Bridgnorth – Telford road, half a mile from Bridgnorth Low Town. GR723934.

Public Transport: Bus services from Wellington and Telford (9/99) and from Wolverhampton (890) stopping at Bridgnorth Low Town. More limited service (436/437) from Shrewsbury and Much Wenlock to Bridgnorth High Town. For something a little different there is the Severn Valley Railway running between Kidderminster and Bridgnorth with various stops *en route*.

SHORT START (page 65): The Davenport Arms, Worfield, three miles west of Bridgnorth off the A 454 Wolverhampton road. GR758956

Public Transport: Bus service 890 Bridgnorth/Wolverhampton stops near to Worfield (Worfield Turn) on the A454. Less regular services from Bridgnorth (67/113) stop in Worfield.

TERRAIN: Gently undulating countryside bordering the River Worfe and through scenic woods and parkland popular with local walkers. One steepish climb at the start, otherwise mainly easy going. Walk at any time although some paths could be overgrown in summer.

THE PUB: The Davenport Arms is the archetypal local. A small brick and tile building in a road of cottages having a bar and lounge serving Banks's and periodic guest beers such as Woods Special and Fullers. You might though be tempted to try the Landlord's own home made ale. Basically furnished but comfortable. *No food. Closed at lunchtimes in the week.*

If you are walking during the week in summer you may wish to start at the Davenport Arms to take advantage of evening opening from 7 p.m. Alternatively, a short diversion from Worfield onto the A454 will bring you to The Wheel which is open at lunchtimes in the week during the summer months.

WALK to the main road and turn left along the grass verge for 100 yards before crossing to take the lane opposite signed 'Cemetery'. After about 250 yards you will reach the cemetery which is not only huge but stated to be 'a prime site for nature conservation which, in the opinion of Shropshire Wildlife Trust, is significant in the county by virtue of its wildlife and geography'. The lowland heath and grassland found here are amongst the rarest habitats in the county making it a very important place for over 120 species of flowering plants. Have a look around if you wish, then return to the entrance and take the steps up to the left of the site. This is quite a stiff climb with some steep steps but it soon levels out and you come to a stile.

Cross the stile and turn right on a path around the top edge of the cemetery, keeping the fence and tree boundary on your right. After the end of the cemetery the path loops left before entering Hermitage Wood, through which you climb steadily on a well defined path until arriving at a junction on level ground where you swing left to walk along the top edge of the wood. A further 150 yards will bring you to a fork and here bear right to a stile which can be seen at the edge of the trees.

Having negotiated the stile turn left following the edge of a field as it borders the wood, go through a gap in a crossing fence and enter the next field. Follow the left boundary as it moves away from the wood to pass through a waymarked gate, then cross the ensuing field as directed aiming

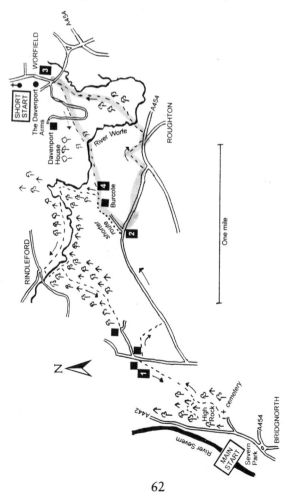

between two cottages in view on the opposite side. In the far corner is a stile. **1**

Cross the stile onto a lane turning right then almost immediately left up a waymarked stone driveway alongside one of the cottages. At the end of the driveway take the right of two facing gates and proceed into a field with a fence and tree boundary on your left. About 50 yards from the end of the field follow the waymark right, across the field to reach a waymarked gate. Go through this to walk along a broad grassy path which exits through a timber gate onto a lane. Turn left along the lane and continue on it for a total distance of about a mile as it passes through a quiet rural backwater. Along the way, after going round a long right bend, you will pass the entrance to Burcote House on your left from which direction those on the short walk will exit onto the lane. **2**

Continue on the lane (or turn left onto it if on the short walk) as it descends towards the main A454 but, immediately before reaching it, there is a gateway on your left. Go through the gate into a field with a fence boundary on the right. After a short distance the ground dips slightly and after a further 100 yards there is a stile on the right underneath two willow trees. Cross this and follow a waymark diagonally right to a stile on the opposite boundary. You are now facing the main road again – cross the stile and climb an embankment onto a grass verge alongside the road. Bear left along it – but only for about 75 yards you will be relieved to know! – until crossing another stile on your left taking you across the same field you have just come out of! A little odd you might think but nevertheless correct and you have avoided what would otherwise have been a longer walk along the main road.

Cross a stile at the far side of the field and a footbridge over the River Worfe (the first of several occasions when you will cross the river) and, once over, bear very slightly right towards a gate in front of the wood ahead. There is also a stile here to cross before branching immediately left at a fork to follow a well defined path through the wood of mixed deciduous trees. Ignore all side paths as the way descends to exit the wood at a stile which you cross and then bear half left across pasture aiming to the left of a line of trees bordering the River Worfe where you cross another stile. Now continue forward across a field to a gate and a road sign that you can see on the far side. Beside the gate is another stile bringing you onto a lane. Cross directly up the opposite lane passing a little war memorial and green to arrive at the Davenport Arms after about 100 yards. **3**

WORFIELD. *Now a commuter village, Worfield still retains the picturesque charm associated with days gone by and contains many buildings of considerable character. The Davenport Estate owns the majority of them and it is customary for tenants to pay their rent twice yearly at the Davenport Arms, although I suspect they may use the occasion to indulge in other pursuits. The sandstone church of St. Peter dominates the skyline with its lofty spire rising 200 feet above floor level. There is a legend concerned with the devil's interference with the building of the church, which was to be built at the highest point. The*

devil objected and every night he removed the stones which had been
laid during the day and workmen found them next morning on a lower
site. Tired of trying to overcome this, the workmen eventually gave in
and accepted the new site. The siting appears to have brought no evil
consequences whatsoever!

Don't tarry too long or you might come face to face with the resident ghost! There is a story that some former tenants thought that the pub was haunted because their dog refused to enter one of the rooms and walked around with its tuʌ raised. In fact the pub is known locally as 'The Dog' although I am not sure whether this tale is the origin of the name. Retrace your steps back to the road junction and go over the same stile crossed on the outward route. After 50 yards pass a redundant stile and bear half right diagonally across a field aiming firstly to the left of the first solitary tree, a sweet chestnut, and then towards a solitary oak, thereafter continuing on your line to a stile in the far boundary. When researching this walk I found this field to be planted with 6 ft. high maize and was obliged to take a route around the edge to reach the same point.

Cross over the tarmac driveway leading to Davenport House and climb up an embankment on the other side, at the top of which is a good view over surrounding countryside. Continue your line forward to cross the driveway again. Now on the right you can see Davenport House, a large three storey Georgian residence built in 1726 which dominates the landscape. The round brick structure nearby is the remains of a dovecot with nearly 1000 'pop holes' and dates from about the same time as the house. Descend on a track passing to the left of a lime tree down to a gate. Go through and branch half left to the left of an oak tree 150 yards ahead and on to a small group of trees where there is a footbridge beside an old waterwheel to cross over the River Worfe again.

The 11 ft diameter waterwheel dates from the early nineteenth century and powered a pumping station that took water from a nearby spring up to Davenport House and the surrounding farms and cottages. It was rebuilt in 1952 but was abandoned in 1956 following the death of the owner of Davenport House who had resolutely refused to be connected to the mains supply.

Proceed in the ensuing field with the river on your right and after 150 yards there is another stile. This is somewhat superfluous as there is a large gap to the side of it but continue ahead for another 50 yards to cross a stile on your left into a field. Now bear half right to a gate in the top right corner and go through onto a broad farm track to reach a cottage after some 150 yards. To the left of the cottage is a lovely sandstone barn and adjacent to that a waymarked gate leading to a stile 20 yards further on. **4**

If on the short route the way is straight ahead, otherwise turn right along a narrow path to the rear of the cottage and through attractive fringe woodland above the river with sandstone outcrops on the left. Cross a stile and walk along the edge of a field with a sandstone escarpment on the left and still with the river for company. Follow the escarpment around to the left and negotiate a stile to the left of a gate facing the rear of a cottage. Press forward on a sandstone path and onto a tarmac driveway running to the left of the cottage, over a cattle grid and then a bridge over the river.

Ignore a stile on your left immediately after crossing the bridge and continue on a tarmac driveway for getting on for half a mile through an attractive river plain well known to local walkers. Go through a gate in front of a cottage towards the rural hamlet of Rindleford *but do not exit onto the lane.* You will see a large former mill building – turn left in front of it and don't be put off by 'Private' signs. **5**

You will next cross two footbridges in quick succession and follow a waymarked path through trees with the river now on your left. After some 150 yards, just beyond a sandstone outcrop, say goodbye to the river and turn right up a grassy track between trees. As you cannot fail to have noticed, sandstone is a predominant feature on this walk. It is Permian, formed 260 million years ago and is about 200 metres thick. The cliffs around The Hermitage and High Rock were cut out by glacial floodwaters.

The track winds pleasantly through bracken and semi-heathland and you eventually join and continue ahead along a wider gravelled track. Stay with this for some time until passing through a metal gate in front of a sandstone outbuilding to a house. Join and continue forward on a stone track to exit onto a lane. You are now very close to a point passed on the outward route. Turn left onto the lane and almost immediately cross a stile on the right into a field which you should recognise from the early part of the walk.

Now simply follow the outward route in reverse back to the start. In case you have forgotten, bear half left across the field towards the left edge of the tree line ahead. Go through a metal gate into the next field and through a gap in a crossing hedge. After about 100 yards cross a stile on the right into the wood and almost immediately go left at a junction of paths. There is an interesting diversion from here down to High Rock where you can experience stunning views over Bridgnorth and the Severn Valley. To get there take a sharp right path about 75 yards after entering the wood and follow a winding path through the woods for around a third of a mile. The path is narrow in parts and can be slippery in wet weather so take great care. Retrace your steps to the turn off point from the upper path and continue on it until reaching the next fork where you turn right downhill to the cemetery and the car park.

SHORTER WALK

FROM the Davenport Arms, point 3, follow the main route through to point 4. After crossing the stile take the path straight ahead gradually climbing through trees. At the top of the incline the path turns to grass passing between hedgerows and after 40 yards loops left along a farm track to exit onto the main drive to Burcote Farm. Turn right down the drive and , on reaching a lane at point 2, bear left and follow the main route again to point 3 and the pub.

13
The Stiperstones and Norbury

FACT*file*

MAPS: Landranger 137; Pathfinder 909

DISTANCES: 8¼ miles; shorter walk 3¼ miles

MAIN START: The Cranberry Rock car park, the most convenient starting point for most walks in the Stiperstones area. From the Shrewsbury direction, take the A488 Bishops Castle road for about 14 miles and after passing through Hope Valley, take a left turn through Shelve and follow the lanes to Cranberry Rock. The same turning is some seven miles north of Bishops Castle except of course it is on the right from this direction. A map would be useful if you don't know your way around.GR 369976.

Public Transport: Nothing suitable.

SHORT START (page 71): The Sun at Norbury, four miles north-east of Bishops Castle off the A488 or the A489 Craven Arms Road. GR364928.

Public Transport: Very limited bus service 762 from Bishops Castle (Tues only) calling at Norbury.

TERRAIN: There are plenty of walks over the main Stiperstones Rocks so I am avoiding these and taking you through the less well known Stiperstones Wood to the south and on over Linley Hill into the village of Norbury. This is a strenuous walk but the views are spectacular. Walk at any time but beware in the winter months as the weather conditions can change rapidly – go well equipped.

THE PUB: The Sun at Norbury is very close to my ideal pub – cosy, comfortable, friendly and with lots of character. Serving Worthington, Murphy's, Carlsberg and draught cider together with bar snacks and meals in a separate restaurant. If you want to eat there is a mouth-watering menu.

Lunch-time opening on Sundays and Bank Holidays only.

If you are walking Tues-Sat in the summer you may wish to start from The Sun to take advantage of evening opening from 7 p.m. (except Mons).

FROM the car park return to the lane and cross a stile opposite onto a grassy track through gorse to reach a ramshackle collection of farm buildings. The waymarked route between outbuildings is sometimes fenced off and I found it necessary to skirt around to the right through a gateway into a field at the rear containing old farm machinery. Proceed through into the next field and prepare yourself for a little muddy going for a while.

At the end of the field is a waymarked stile with a choice of routes –

66

cross and take a line more or less straight ahead, ignoring the stile on the left, through a scrubby tree area and over a brook into another field with a post and wire boundary on your left. There is a further stile 80 yards ahead where the ground around can be very boggy as a stream runs in front of it!

Having negotiated this, continue the line forward over a short section of field towards a dip 100 yards in front. In the dip is a stream which you are obliged to cross before climbing an embankment and onwards to a stile exiting onto a lane after another 25 yards. Turn left on the lane which descends to pass a pretty stone cottage on the right, then another cottage on a left hand bend, immediately after which is a waymarked stile on the right.

This leads onto a grassy track between fences to a fence stile 100 yards ahead and you cross this into a field with the boundary on your left, heading uphill towards Stiperstones Wood. The way loops right to a waymarked fence stile in front of the wood. Cross this and a short section of scrub onto a forestry track but be careful not to follow the waymark post directing right; instead bear left along the track. **1**

There are super views to the left over the surrounding hills before you meet and continue ahead along another track which follows the bottom edge of the wood. After a while the track enters the wood whereupon you have to scramble down a short embankment onto a narrower path strewn with pine needles. You will pass a waymark post leading you into a denser

67

part of the wood where you pick your way through the trees to reach another waymark post.

Continue ahead here but very slightly left and this leads you onto a sunken track at or close to a further waymark. Walk along the sunken track for a distance of about 100 yards, depending upon the exact point of entry onto it, and you will arrive at a waymark in front of a broader track. This is the Shropshire Way and you turn left onto it to descend on an attractive course through the trees to exit via a stile onto a tarmac lane.

Bear right here then immediately left over another stile following the Shropshire Way and Wild Edric's Way marks. Wild Edric was a legendary character who led local resistance to the Norman invasion. Eventually he came to terms with William, much to the distaste of his followers, and he was banished. His death was never recorded and many legends grew around him. Whenever his ghostly form is seen galloping furiously over the hills it is said to be a portent of impending war.

Proceed straight down the centre of the field towards a tree line in the valley where you may be able to see a footbridge. Over to the right is Heath Mynd and ahead Linley Hill, which is our immediate destination. There is a little stream in the field to cross before reaching the footbridge and, after the latter, is a double stile and a steepish embankment to negotiate before exiting onto another lane.

Turn right on the lane which bends round to pass Ridge Farm, shortly after which is a waymark post and gate on your left. Go through and climb up through a field with the boundary on the left. Ignore a gate on the left and continue a fairly stiff upward course until almost at the top where a look backwards will I hope convince you that the effort was worthwhile. There is a magnificent view from here over the rocky outcrops of Stiperstones and surrounding features.

STIPERSTONES. *Perhaps I should say a few things about these wild, dramatic and mysterious outcrops of rock, the highest point of which is 1760 feet above sea level. It forms part of a National Nature Reserve encompassing an area of outstanding natural beauty with deep valleys and quartz like ridges which glint in the sun like jewels. Formed by volcanic eruption 480 million years ago, the area was once intensively mined for lead and other deposits and many remains of this industry can be seen today. The area is rich in folklore including tales of Wild Edric and the Devil.*

At the top of the climb cross a stile in front of a small wood onto a track but after about 30 yards leave it and bear right along the left boundary of the wood following waymarks. Continue to a point some 70 yards before a crossing fence, go over a stile on your right and, having done so, bear half left across a short section of field to meet the same crossing fence a little further along. Turn right here and follow the fence on your left to cross a stile to the side of a metal gate. Some 15 yards further on is a waymarked timber gate on the left which is the exit point on the short route. **2**

Continue past, or turn left if on the short route, to follow a post and wire boundary across the top of Linley Hill with great views on both sides and you shortly join a line of mature beech trees with Heath Mynd, Cefn Gunthly and Black Rhadley Hill all visible to the right. Go through a waymarked gate after which gradually move away from the line of trees towards a stile in a crossing fence ahead to the left of a gate. Continue your line forward to join another line of beech trees. It is in fact an avenue planted by unemployed soldiers after the Napoleonic Wars and the unfortunate effects of age and decay are clear to see. Many of the dead trees have been replaced but it will be a long time before the avenue is restored to its former splendour. Go through a gate and descend to cross a stile to the right of another gate. As the descent becomes more gradual you go through a timber gate in front of a fir wood and after 20 yards bear left over a waymarked stile onto a rough farm track. **3**

The track leads to the left of a cottage which you may have spotted coming down the hill and you go over a stile, through a gate keeping on the track as it winds around the left of some farm buildings to reach another stile. There is a choice of routes here – take the left turn along a defined track which soon peters out at a point where the left fence turns 90 degrees, and here you branch half right down and across a field to a footbridge close to the bottom corner.

Once over the footbridge proceed on the same line in the next field aiming for a small tree which sticks up above the rest. Here there is a crossing fence and we turn left in front of it. Ignore the first gate on the right but cross a stile to the right of a second gate and bear half left over the field towards some farm buildings with Norbury in view further to the left. There is a stile to the left of the buildings; go over this and continue ahead along a track and through a waymarked gate. The track passes to the right of a silage store and after a while turns stony and drops down into Norbury. Turn left on reaching a lane and follow it around to The Sun. **4**

NORBURY. A small rural settlement with sheep and cattle rearing the main activities, built in a fortress-like pattern with the buildings forming a square round the outside of the churchyard. In common with similar villages it has suffered a population decline – from 412 in 1861 down to a mere 43 today. It still manages to support a pub however although I suspect not without the assistance of 'outsiders' and the school serves a number of outlying parishes. The Church of All Saints is beautiful and contains a number of interesting features including an unusual painted ceiling, attractive stained glass and a fine organ. A huge yew tree in the churchyard is over 33 feet in circumference and is reputed to be one of the ten oldest trees in the country.

The urge to linger in The Sun may be difficult to overcome but, on the assumption that you will succeed, turn right and retrace your steps for a few yards to a phone box where you turn right again along a narrow tarmac lane. After 100 yards there is a turning left for those on the shorter route but continue on the lane as it ascends gradually and then more steeply.

The Sun, Norbury

Now, pay particular attention here! The lane goes through a series of bends and after a total distance of about three quarters of a mile you need to go left through a short cutting to a metal gate to the right of an ash tree. Not the first gate by an ash tree at the end of a stone wall but the second, almost identical, situation a little further on. This gate leads onto a well defined track to the right of further ash trees and shortly loops right and rises. You will pass through a gate onto a broad grassy track and then through another gate to continue the climb.

As the ground levels off ignore a stile in the post and wire fence coming in from the right but continue forward parallel with this fence. The panoramic views from here will not escape your notice. Backwards you can see the Long Mynd in the distance on a clear day and ahead the brooding crags of the Stiperstones again. You go through a bit of a marshy area before the path starts to rise again and after another gate it becomes less well defined.

The fence is still there on your right as the way shortly begins to descend and passes through some more marshy ground beyond which is a gate in the far right field corner. This gate may not be visible until you almost get to it; go through and continue to follow the same boundary but to the right of it for only about 100 yards to take a stile on the left into a field. Bear slightly left away from the fence to a gap in a crossing fence to the left of a water trough 200 yards or so ahead and continue to the top of a short rise.

At this point you can see Cold Hill Farm in the valley in front of you and to get to it you need to veer half left down the other side of the rise to a waymarked gate in the bottom left corner of the field. Go through, turning right into the next field with a fence on your right, cross a stile in front of the farmhouse and bear left to follow a track across the rear of it.

Keep tight on the fence to exit onto a lane via a hidden fence stile to the right of a holly hedge. **5**

Turn right, then left after 200 yards along a broad track between hedgerows and cross a stile by a gate into a field with a mixed tree boundary on your left. Where this loops left after 50 yards continue your line directly forward across and up the centre of the field to a stile 120 yards ahead in a crossing boundary. Cross this and turn right to follow the bottom edge of a hill with a post and wire boundary on your right.

As you get towards the end of the hill look for a stile in the right boundary to the left of a metal gate but DO NOT CROSS IT. Instead bear almost due left up the field along to the right of the hill and you will meet the end of a broad track where there is a waymark post directing you right onto it. At the top is another post with a choice of routes – go right and after a few yards cross a fence stile, then another immediately on your left. Now head across a scrubby field, crossing a stream in the middle, to a stile in the crossing boundary ahead.

Once in the next field continue with the boundary on your right to go over another stile at the far end. Proceed towards farm buildings but only for about 30 yards before turning left through a gap in the boundary hedge, then bear half right to cross a stile after another 30 yards (*this field was thistly when I last walked through and I found it less painful to go round the edge!*). Bear half right to yet another stile after 20 yards. This you may recognise as a stile crossed on the early part of the walk and you now simply retrace your steps back to the car park.

SHORTER WALK

STARTING from The Sun at Norbury, with your back to the pub turn right then right again by a phone box along a lane. After 100 yards bear left along another lane which rises gradually at first, then more steeply after a cottage on the left. After a while it levels out and there are smashing views over the valley and the Long Mynd beyond.

Keep on the lane as it swings left and starts to rise again with the views getting better and better. The lane swings right, crosses a cattle grid and continues onward and upward. Eventually it levels out again but then returns to its upward direction and turns to stone as it passes the entrance to Clapper Farm. The ascent becomes more gradual with some stunning views in prospect and you pass through a metal gate to enter moorland.

The way leads around the right side of Norbury Hill, then levels out and becomes more grassy after which it actually descends a little. You can now see Stiperstones Woods ahead and the rocky outcrops of the main ridge over to the half right. You will shortly arrive at a timber gate, which is point 2 on the main route, and here turn left and follow the main route through to point 4.

14

Dudmaston

FACT*file*

MAPS: Landranger 138 Pathfinder 932

DISTANCES: 7½ miles; shorter walk 3¾ miles

MAIN START: Car park at Hampton Loade. To get there from Bridgnorth take the A442 Kidderminster road and one mile after passing through Quatt turn right along a signposted lane. GR747866.

Public Transport: Train: Severn Valley Railway, Bridgnorth/Kidderminster stopping at Hampton Loade. From Hampton Loade station it is necessary to cross the River Severn by ferry which, at the time of writing, was operating daily from 11 a.m. It would probably be wise to check with Kidderminster Tourist Office (01562 829400) that the service is still available. Bus: No services. However, the 297 service (Bridgnorth/Kidderminster, Mon-Sat) stops at Quatt so you could start your walk from there.

SHORT START (page 76): The Cider House at Wooton. From Bridgnorth take the A458 Stourbridge road and after 3½ miles turn right towards Quatt then immediately left on a country lane, over crossroads after half a mile and the pub is on your left after a further a quarter of a mile. It can be approached from the Stourbridge direction by turning left about three quarters of a mile after passing through Six Ashes. GR773888.

Public Transport: No services to Wooton. However, the 297 service (Bridgnorth/Kidderminster, Mon-Sat) stops at Quatt so you could start your walk from there.

TERRAIN: Easy walking through scenic parkland, rural villages and along the River Severn. Walk at any time although some paths can get overgrown in summer and fields may be planted.

THE PUBS: The Cider House, Wooton: One of the most unusual pubs you are likely to find, selling cider, spirits and soft drinks only – and no food other than snacks. Located in an isolated rural hamlet, the building is of suitably rustic appearance and has one large bar with wood burning stove and two smaller ones, one of them having a cast iron range and large display of ceiling mounted mugs. Cider is available in glass or jar and you can choose from Strongbow in various strengths up to 7½%, Scrumpy Jack, Old Traditional, Kingsacre Special Reserve and others. One of the bars proudly displays an ode to cider as follows: 'Good cider 'tis a drink divine, better by far than all your wine. Good in grief, good in joy – good for maid, man and boy' Not everyone would agree with that I'm sure. Plenty of outside seating. *Normal opening times.*

The Lion Inn, Hampton Loade: If you don't like cider or want some food you may prefer to start at Wooton and break at the Lion. This family run inn dates from the early 1600s and is one of the village's oldest buildings. It is spacious and has a number of bars and a restaurant boasting a selection of reasonably priced culinary delights. Bar meals and sandwiches also available. On the drinks front you can choose from a number of Real Ales; or how about one of their speciality country wines? Large garden area with seating.
Closed Monday lunch-times and weekday lunch-times during winter.

FROM the car park go through the kissing gate onto a track alongside the River Severn and continue on it for about 1¼ miles. You will pass under a blot of a footbridge and skirt the edge of Long Covert on the right, with a bit of luck experiencing the sight and sounds of the Severn Valley Railway on the other side of the river. As you near the end of the tree belt the path swings right and into fringe vegetation alongside Quatt Brook, which is subsequently crossed via a footbridge. Proceed now with trees on your right climbing gently until reaching a stile on the right by a gateway in front of Rookery Cottage. A look back here will be rewarded with fine views over the Severn flood-plain.

Cross the stile onto a grassy track and a further stile at the far side of the cottage. From this point veer left (do not take the stile on the right into the wood) and soon join a broad sandstone gravel track through parkland to a line of trees ahead. Shortly thereafter the west front of Dudmaston Hall and Dudmaston Big Pool will appear on your right in a magnificent setting.

DUDMASTON HALL AND ESTATE. *Owned and managed by the National Trust since 1978, the Dudmaston Estate comprises some 3000 acres of the Severn Valley, including some of the most attractive parkland in Shropshire. The woodlands are a delight, having been professionally planted and managed by the original estate owners, and the lakes are home to a variety of waterfowl. The Hall itself is of early eighteenth century origin and was formerly the home of Francis Darby of Coalbrookdale. It contains much fine furniture and an unusual collection of Dutch flower paintings. There are beautiful grounds sweeping down to the west side of Big Pool. Open April to September inclusive on Wednesdays and Sundays only, 2.00 - 5.30.*

Eventually the surface of the track changes from gravel to tarmac to reach a T-junction by Lodge Farm, where you turn right towards mature trees ahead and the A442. Immediately before reaching the main road there is a stile on your right by a gate – cross this and follow the path left to come out a little further along the road opposite a short flight of steps leading into the wood. **1**

Cross the road carefully and climb the steps, then, shortly after entering the wood, bear left onto a broader crossing track. Turn right at a waymark along a clear path running along the edge of a clearing. This clearing has

73

recently been re-planted to widen the diversity of species and age amongst the estate trees; the tall dead stumps having been deliberately left for raptors to perch on. Go over a crossing track and, a short distance after the path swings left, turn right and descend into Comer Wood where the oldest trees are remnants of the ancient forest of Morfe which once covered the Severn Valley. At the base of the incline is a crossing path where you turn right and then almost immediately left to enter a path running alongside three pools called Brim, Seggy and Wall in order.

This section of the route by the pools (a permissive path, courtesy of the National Trust) is a beautiful, peaceful place to stop awhile to appreciate the surroundings and reflect. Note the variety of trees including the large beech beside Seggy, about 160 years old, and the California Redwoods beyond Wall Pool. When ready, continue forward and after about a quarter of a mile you will reach a stile at the edge of the wood. Cross and turn right onto a broad very sandy track and then left after 60 yards following a waymark into a field with a hedged boundary on the left. As the boundary kinks slightly left after100 yards strike half right across the centre of the field to reach a stile on the opposite boundary and turn left onto a lane. **2**

After 100 yards or so you will find a broad grassy track on the right leading down towards a wood. Follow this as it narrows to a gravel path running alongside the edge of the wood. Immediately before it is joined from the right by a brook, the path rises to the left, narrows further and

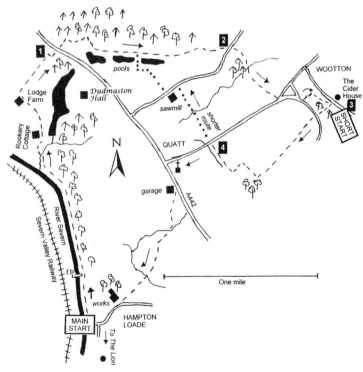

runs parallel to the brook to a plank footbridge. Cross this and climb gently through the trees on the other side until coming to a junction with a road.

Go straight over on a tarmac lane, ignoring a turning to the left but 20 yards further on cross a stile in a tall hedge on the left. Walk along the left field edge and where it kinks left continue your line forward to the right of an electricity pole to a copse, where there is a stile. Cross this and a plank footbridge to follow a narrow winding path through trees and after about 150 yards cross another stile bearing half right across a field. Aim to the right of a clump of trees where you will find a stile into a small car park opposite the Cider House. **3**

If you are a cider drinker you will know that some of it is strong stuff. If not, be warned! Assuming that you are still capable, return to the stile at the rear of the small car park but continue straight forward with a hedge on your left towards the wood. Cross a stile into it and descend a steep bank to a footbridge (around which the ground can be boggy) and a further stile. Cross and climb the embankment on the far side to enter a field where houses come into view. These houses are in fact rather attractive barn conversions and the path leads through a gateway between them to reach a lane.

Cross the lane directly onto a broad track and follow it for about half a mile. On a clear day there are good views over rolling countryside and the Clee Hills to the right. Ignore a clear track going off to the right and carry on until you reach a junction just before a small wood. Here turn right along a field edge with a line of oak and ash trees on your left. The path bears left then right following the line of a brook and exits onto a crossing lane via a gateway. **4**

Turn left along the lane for a quarter of a mile into the village of Quatt and its junction with the A442.

QUATT. *A large proportion of the village is owned by the Dudmaston Estate (i.e. the National Trust) which takes particular care to preserve its essential characteristics. Indeed, most of the inhabitants have some association with the village or the Estate and are equally keen to ensure its long term survival. The red brick tower of St. Andrews Church is very prominent. It was built in 1763 although most of the building is much older. Internally there are numerous monuments to previous owners of Dudmaston. Along the main road is a particularly fine row of Victorian estate cottages which apparently were built to the highest standards of the time.*

Cross the main road carefully and turn left in front of the estate cottages and immediately after passing Quatt Service Station there is a stile by a gate leading into a field. Cross and proceed diagonally to a stile to the right of an oak tree. After crossing this follow the field edge for 50 yards to negotiate a further stile into a field with a hedge on the right. You will shortly go over a plank footbridge and stile before turning right into a meadow to follow a line with trees and a brook on your right. The path gradually moves away from the brook towards a gate in the hedge on the

75

opposite side of the field and here you cross a stile onto a grassy track. After 20 yards it swings left to cross the centre of a field ahead towards a wood.

Pass through a gap in the crossing hedge and turn 90 degrees right to a stile 50 yards ahead. Now bear left into a small field with a wood on the right where the path curves to the right following the edge of the tree line as waymarked. It soon dips to cross a footbridge and continues up some steps to a stile on the other side of the trees. Cross this and the next field to meet a hedged boundary with a large factory on the right and a group of green asphalt roofed houses on the left. Cross a stile in the field corner and over the access road to the factory to a further stile and, after negotiating this, turn left into a field and follow its edge around two sides to emerge onto a lane. Turn right in front of farm buildings and continue on the lane down to Hampton Loade and the starting point.

HAMPTON LOADE. *An attractive hamlet bisected by the River Severn and once a busy port and an important river crossing. You can still cross the river today on a rope ferry and walk up to the Severn Valley Railway Station. During the 1800s it was renowned as an iron forge and in fact was the only one in the world using peat as a fuel and water power for bellows to superheat the furnaces. Severn barges brought in the raw materials and took away the finished products. It was known then as Hampton Load Forge, without an 'e' but was eventually eclipsed by Abraham Darby's Ironbridge Works using coal to smelt iron.*

If wishing to visit the Lion Inn, or indeed if choosing it as the *en route* hostelry, turn left following directional signs along a narrow street between cottages, past former mill buildings until you reach the pub.

SHORTER WALK

FROM the Cider House, point 3, follow the main walk to point 4 and the exit onto a lane. Instead of turning left into Quatt, cross the lane onto a broad farm track along the edge of a field following the National Trust waymark. Stay on it as it loops left then right, ignoring a stile into a field, and at the rear of Old Hall it dips to cross a brook by trees then rises to meet another lane. Turn left here passing Dudmaston Sawmill where many of the stiles in the Shropshire countryside are made and opposite the main entrance take a stile in a hedge on the right.

Follow the field edge for 20 yards, cross another stile on your left turning right to follow a waymark along field edge with hedge on right. The path dips towards trees and Wall pool comes into view. Immediately in front of it the path turns 90 degrees left to follow the bottom edge of the field and brings you to the end of the pool where there is a narrow path right between two oak trees. This takes you to a stile and a path between Wall and Seggy pools. On reaching the other side turn right and pick up the main route at the beginning of the paragraph before point 2 on page 74 and follow through to point 3 and the start.

15
Trysull and Bratch Locks

FACT*file*

MAPS: Landranger 138/139; Pathfinder 912

DISTANCES: 8¾ miles; shorter walk 3¼ miles

MAIN START: On the B4176 Dudley-Bridgnorth Road two miles west of Wombourne. Park at pull-in at the base of path up Abbots Castle Hill. From the Wombourne direction keep on the B4176 as it turns right opposite Swindon Golf Club and the parking spot is on the right after half a mile. From the Bridgnorth direction pass through Upper Aston after which Abbots Castle Hill comes in from the left and look for the parking spot as the base of the ridge meets the road. GR835929

>   **Public Transport:** Very limited bus service (585/6/7) from Wolverhampton stops at Seisdon and Trysull and you could start the walk from one of these points. However, there is a good service (256) between Wolverhampton and Stourbridge stopping at Wombourne and you could then start your walk from Bratch Locks. Leave the bus at the junction of Bratch Lane and Bullmeadow Lane and walk along Bratch Lane to the locks.

SHORT START (page 81): The Plough, located to the south of Trysull village centre. GR852939.

>   **Public Transport:** See above.

TERRAIN: Varied. Includes a section of the Staffs & Worcs Canal with award winning locks, an elevated ridge, farmland and villages. No steep climbs. Can be walked at any time but some paths may be overgrown or cropped in summer.

THE PUB: The Plough is an olde-worlde local which has not been spoilt by a little 'modernisation'. A Banks's house with guest beers usually available plus Guinness and a range of lagers and ciders. Bar snacks and meals; plenty of outside seating for fine days. *Normal opening times.*

WITH your back to the road proceed up the gradual incline of Abbots Castle Hill along a section of the Staffordshire Way, which initially runs parallel with the B4176 before moving away from it. This two mile escarpment of pebble beds forms part of the county boundary and there is evidence of Anglo-Saxon settlement. Indeed the village name of Seisdon which you will enter shortly means 'Hill of the Saxon'. There are good views from various points, particularly from level ground at the top, over Wombourne, Dudley and the fringes of Wolverhampton.

Continue ahead at the waymark on the Staffordshire Way and you will eventually pass a modern green barn with Tinkers Castle Farm on the right (just over a mile from the start). Shortly after that the path goes to the right of Tinkers Castle itself – not a castle in the true sense of the word but probably dating from the late eighteenth century with a cellar incorporating an earlier rock dwelling – to exit onto a lane. Turn right and after a descent of about 300 yards bear left down a tarmac driveway to Wolmore Farm, still on the Staffordshire Way.

As the drive starts to swing left after 250 yards or so there is a bridleway sign on your right which you follow into a field on a narrow path along the left edge. It squiggles left then right to pass well to the left of a large chicken farm and takes you through a gate onto a broader track running alongside 'Woodcote' and more farm buildings. The track arrives at some private houses with an M.E.B. substation on your left. Turn left here for about 70 yards to reach a junction with Fox Road. **1**

Turn left then immediately right down Post Office Road and through a pleasant mixed residential area bordering the village of Seisdon. After a

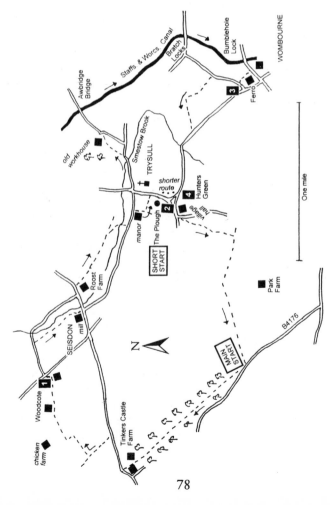

78

third of a mile on reaching cottage No.135, just before the lane bends right, take the waymarked kissing gate on the right into a field. Cross directly to go through another kissing gate and in the next field keep to the left boundary by Smestow Brook to reach a third kissing gate. In the next field continue with the boundary on your left parallel with the brook and on the far side climb some steps and go through kissing gate No.4.

Now walk along a path verging the bottom of some private gardens to exit via a gate onto a service road. Cross directly and over a stile between brick walls onto a path to the left of a large white painted period residence known as The Mill House. On reaching a lane turn left over a bridge, ignore a turning to the left which is the other end of Post Office Road, and after a further 100 yards bear right along an enclosed broad track immediately after Roost Farm.

The track opens out by some farm buildings and you continue on for about 175 yards before going through an easily missed waymarked kissing gate in the hedge on your right into a field. Bear half left aiming towards a large horse chestnut tree, to the right of which is a stile. Note the ancient brick bridge over a stream which is the old mill leat to The Mill House passed a little earlier. No need to cross the stile – there is a gap to the side of it – then continue ahead over a field to cross a footbridge and go through a kissing gate to exit onto a lane linking Seisdon and Trysull.

Turn left and after 150 yards branch off right along a driveway immediately after Trysull Manor which, as the name implies, is a property of grand proportions and dates from 1653. Pass to the left of some outbuildings and go through a gate. As the track opens out into a field turn left along the field edge and at the end continue forward between paddocks to go through another gate leading down to a lane. Turn right here and The Plough is on your right after about 75 yards. **2**

Parting company with the Plough may present some difficulty but after succeeding retrace your steps down the lane past the point of exit onto it a little earlier (or a lot earlier depending on how long you spent in the pub) and continue into the village of Trysull.

TRYSULL & SEISDON. *Lying within the commuter belt of the Black Country towns the two villages have a combined population of about 1000. Seisdon is mentioned in the Domesday Book and gave its name to the County Hundred in Saxon times; indeed it was only after a recent change in Local Government structure that it ceased to be the administrative centre for quite a large area. The old Court House still stands. Trysull contains a number of interesting buildings, not the least of which is All Saints Church. Most of the present structure originates from the thirteenth and fourteenth centuries although it has been extended and altered at various other times. The parish chest just inside the entrance dates from the 1100s and is reputed to be one of the finest in the country and together with other artefacts makes this pretty church well worth a visit. Apparently the church has a bequest that* *the verger is paid one pound per year to keep the congregation awake during sermons!*

At the crossroads turn right past The Bell and a cottage with the curious name of 'Ovens End' and over a bridge, shortly after which the lane swings right. On the left is a gap in the hedgerow right on the bend – go through this and follow a trodden path across the field which gently rises over a small hummock. At the far side is The Old Workhouse, thankfully no longer in use although you might be able to imagine what life must have been like there.

Continue forward to meet and proceed ahead along a lane for about a quarter of a mile to arrive at Awbridge Bridge. Cross it and turn left and under the bridge onto the towpath of the Staffs & Worcs Canal. There is a lock here but you will see more of interest at Bratch which is reached after about a mile.

Bratch locks

BRATCH LOCKS *are an unusual three lock flight which takes the canal through a vertical interval of 30 ft. They were re-opened in 1994 after complete restoration and an information board provides all the details. The small octagonal building is a former tollhouse with an ornamental central chimney and, nearby, you can see the Victorian Waterworks which is one of a number along the canal and contains engines fired by coal ferried along it. The canal itself was built by James Brindley and was part of his scheme for linking the Trent & Mersey with the River Severn.*

Stay on the towpath as it goes under a road and past Bumblehole Lock to the next bridge by the Round Oak pub. Go under the bridge and turn right to meet a road where you bear left then immediately right up a tarmac driveway opposite the premises of Stein Atkinson Stordy to find some metal gates in front of a factory unit. Take the narrow path to the left of it around the edge of the Ferro premises to exit onto a lane. **3**

Turn right and follow the lane past a row of semi-detached houses in an elevated position overlooking the canal and new development beyond. Some 200 yards after the houses end look for a stile on your left under a holly tree and cross into a field following the left boundary. Go over another stile in a crossing fence and continue with the hedge in the next field but about three quarters of the way along it take a stile on the left to follow another hedged boundary on your right. At the end of this field is a further stile to negotiate after which bear right onto Woodford Lane. The lane takes you over Smestow Brook again and leads out at the top end of Trysull by Hunters Green. **4**

Bear left at the fork alongside Woodford House and left again on reaching a lane. This loops left after passing the village hall and directly opposite on the bend is a waymarked stile on your right. Cross into a long field following the left boundary. Half-way along it dog-legs right then left and you continue on the same line to reach a stile in front of a broad track. Turn right here. As the right-hand boundary disappears the track opens out into a field where you continue forward, ignoring a gap on the left after a few yards leading to Park Farm.

A little directional care is called for now. Proceed on your line but look over to the half left and note three trees close together in a crossing boundary between adjacent fields. These are your destination and, to get there, about 150 yards past the gap to the farm you are funnelled between holly hedges into the adjacent field. You then continue the line forward across the field on a narrow track heading for the three trees, effectively cutting off the right hand corner of the field. Please note that this track might be ploughed up on occasions and the three trees do not appear as such from this angle!

Before reaching them you will come to a boundary hedge between two fields – follow the right side past the three trees, and at the end of the field cross a track then a footbridge and stile. Cross the next field directly aiming immediately to the left of an electricity pole and continue the line beyond it towards a row of trees ahead. When arriving at the trees there is a stile with a gap to the side – go through this and on meeting the road bear right for 50 yards back to the start.

SHORTER WALK

STARTING from The Plough, point 2, follow the main route to Hunters Green and point 4. Bear right at the fork and then right again on reaching the lane for 100 yards or so to return to the pub.

FACT*file*

MAPS: Landranger 137; Pathfinder 931

DISTANCES: 7 miles; shorter walk 3¾ miles

MAIN START: In the village of Tugford which is approached from the B4368 Bridgnorth-Craven Arms road via a left turn down a narrow country lane from Beambridge, one mile on the Bridgnorth side of Munslow (or a right turn if travelling from the Craven Arms direction). There is verge parking by the church or telephone kiosk. GR556872

Public Transport: Very limited. Bus services 713/715 from Bridgnorth call at Tugford. Alternatively, services 154/155/156/538/712/713/715 Ludlow/Bridgnorth call at Beambridge, about one mile from Broncroft Castle (*see map*) and you may wish to start from there.

SHORT START (page 87): From the Tally Ho at Bouldon which is also reached from the same turn at Beambridge or from the east on the lanes joining the village with Diddlebury about three miles away. GR543852

Public Transport: As above, services 713/715 call at Bouldon. Also limited service 716 from Ludlow on schooldays only.

TERRAIN: Undulating country with a few short climbs but nothing too strenuous. Good views over the Clees and Wenlock Edge and several places of interest *en route* including the picturesque village of Clee St. Margaret. In summer some of the paths can be overgrown and fields cropped.

THE PUB: A simple pub in a pleasant setting, the Tally Ho is an ideal stop for walkers. It is a Free House with two bars and a small restaurant. Bar snacks are available. Ales include Burton, Ansells, Tetley, Carlsberg , Kilkenny Irish and Guinness. *Normal opening times.*

BEFORE starting out have a look at Tugford Church (St. Catherines). Some of the original Norman features remain and the unusual choir gallery is 500 years old. It is a most interesting building with a curious feature – the walls lean inwards or outwards depending on whether you are inside or outside. With your back to the church take the lane in front of you signed Broadstone, Holdgate and Stanton Long. Ignore a turning right after which the lane ascends, and as it levels out there is a metal gate in the hedge on your left.

Go through into a field and cross, aiming for three oak trees ahead, gradually closing with a hedge coming in from the right. There is a farm below on the left and good views over the village with the woods beyond. Pass the three trees and continue to close gradually with the hedge along a ridge to a fence stile in the top right corner. Cross this and turn 90 degrees right into a field following the boundary. Over on the left you can see Broncroft Castle in the trees but you will get a much closer look a little later. As the ground levels expansive views open up towards Wenlock Edge and you pass through a gap into the next field keeping to the same boundary hedge.

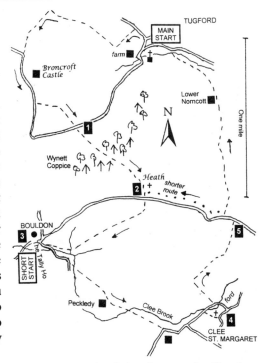

Go through another gap, passing to the left of some derelict farm buildings and on approaching the field corner there is a fence stile just off to the left. This stile is a bit on the high side but, having negotiated it, bear left onto a narrow track between trees. The track winds along for about a third of a mile and descends to reach a junction with a lane. Parts of it can get boggy or overgrown at times so it is to be hoped you're wearing sensible footwear!

Turn left on the lane and follow it over a bridge and around the front of Broncroft Castle. This splendid stone built residence with its castellated towers and manicured lawns has a most comfortable ambience – the sort of place for me if I win the National Lottery. I could tell you quite a lot about it if space permitted but will merely say that it was originally a fourteenth century fortress and the scene of some fighting and despoliation during the Civil War. It was completely restored and added to in the nineteenth century.

About 100 yards after passing the rear entrance there is a driveway on the left leading to some cottages. Look for a stile to the right of it into a field and, once in , gradually move away from the left boundary to pass between two oaks and a single oak to cross a stile in the corner ahead. The official right of way is now half right across the field to a further stile in the top left corner (*but I found it more practical to turn left and follow the edge around to the same point*). The stile exits onto a lane which you cross almost directly to another stile on the other side. **1**

Cross the stile and ascend towards Wynett Coppice following the right

83

Broncroft Castle

boundary and at the top there is a gate. Stop for a breather and look back over the patchwork quilt of fields on the lower slopes of Wenlock Edge and Corvedale. Go through the gate and bear left in the wood on a narrow path and, on reaching a broader crossing path, bear left again. After some 100 yards branch right on another narrow path uphill. This becomes a little indistinct through the pine trees but continue on your line to pass through a gate on the far side.

Proceed in a level field with a tree line boundary on the right and at the end turn right through a waymarked gate, but after only another 50 yards bear left through a barred gate to follow a hedged boundary on your left in the direction of a church ahead. This boundary kinks left after 70 yards but you continue the line straight ahead across the field to a small gate at the rear of the church. The undulations in this field are all that remain of the medieval village of Heath apart from the church, which as you will see on going through the gate, is a tiny chapel dating from 1090 sitting in the middle of a small field. Services are still held here and a key is available for those who wish to look inside. Go through a gate on the other side onto a lane. **2**

Turn right and after 25 yards bear left over a dilapidated fence stile along a bridleway (how you would get a horse over I do not know!). Pass through a scrubby field with a stone farm wall on your right and, on reaching a farm track, bear right through a barred gate and then through another diagonally opposite into a larger field. The way is right now to follow a hedge and tree boundary on the right and descend, taking in the views of Wenlock Edge.

You will come to two metal gates – take the one on the right and

84

continue downhill now with the boundary on your left. Cross a fence stile before proceeding with the boundary on your right again. After a short distance you arrive at a new plantation of saplings and a small enclosure with a post and wire fence around it and stiles on each side. Cross the enclosure and shortly negotiate a post and wire fence to bear slightly right over a stream and through a barred gate at the bottom taking you into a narrow field bordering Clee Brook. Take the second gate on the right after about 120 yards into the adjacent field, following the same line but now with the hedge on your left. At the end of the field, there are two further gates to pass through before turning right onto a lane. Continue straight on at T-junction until coming to the Tally Ho. **3**

Whilst in the pub do remember that you still have about half of the walk left to do. On leaving, retrace your steps past the two gate exit onto the lane and through an attractive hamlet of stone built cottages and farmhouses. Bouldon Mill is on the left although the mill wheel appears long defunct. Where the tarmac ends continue forward on a track by a cottage and after a few yards bear left at a junction along the lower path. After a further 120 yards, immediately following a right-hand bend, there is a fence stile on the left to cross. If you reach the metal gate you have gone too far!

Head through the field directly towards a tree lined brook to cross a footbridge, climb a short embankment and proceed in a field with a boundary on the left and on the far side you will find two gates. The route is now through the left gate onto a short sunken lane but if this is overgrown in summer take the right gate into a field and follow the same line with the sunken lane on your left.

On reaching Peckledy Farm go through a barred gate onto a track running to the left of the buildings, then through a timber gate and after 30 yards take the left one of two gates onto another sunken path. This path winds through an arbour of mixed trees and exits at another footbridge over Clee Brook. Cross this into a field and follow the boundary and brook on your left before negotiating a stile by a gate with an attractive half timbered black and white cottage directly in view.

Continue ahead aiming for the cottage and cross a stile onto a lane in front of it. Go forward on the lane to the left of the cottage and through a most picturesque area of chocolate box houses in the sort of idyllic setting one always dreams of living. Pass the turning off to Stoke St. Milborough and on reaching 'Carpenters' on your left, hidden in the hedge opposite are some steps up to a fence stile. Cross this and climb a short embankment, from the top of which you can see a church slightly off to the left. Go over a further fence stile into the churchyard, visit the church if you wish (see below) and turn left onto a lane to walk through another part of the gorgeous village of Clee St. Margaret. **4**

CLEE ST. MARGARET. *No one could leave this place without an abiding impression of its charm and immense character. Furthermore it is totally unspoilt – no pub, shops, school, petrol station or even*

85

mains drainage. Do visit the church, it has a wonderful atmosphere. Mainly Norman, it was part of the Wenlock Priory Estate until the Dissolution of the Monasteries. In 1872 it was substantially restored although the south door has been there for over 600 years. There is a placard in the porch with a homily which, religious or not, you might find moving. It certainly puts things into perspective a little.

At a junction of lanes turn left along the road to Ludlow and through what is reputed to be the longest ford in Shropshire. You need not go through it literally as there is a path alongside. Continue for about 150 yards to where the lane bends left and take a right turn up a stony track between hedgerows. After a while the track levels out to continue through trees and bears right. Continue on it as it rises again and takes you through a barred gate, after which there are views of Nordy Bank iron age hill fort on your right. Where the track opens out into a small copse keep left into the corner and go through the right of two metal gates before continuing on the track until it exits onto a lane by a farm. **5**

Turn left and after 150 yards, where the lane begins to bend left, bear right up a stone farm track. Go through a metal gate and at the top of the rise, where there is a dramatic view of Clee Hill, the track winds right – but you go more or less straight ahead over a dilapidated gate with blue and yellow marker tape on it and enter a sunken path between hedgerows. The path can become overgrown in summer and eventually exits into a field with a hedged boundary on the right. Keep the line forward in the field and at the end turn right through a gateway and still keep the same line but now with the field boundary on your left.

After 150 yards the way loops right down along a short green lane and, at the junction with a farm track, bear left crossing a field with another excellent view of Clee Hill on the right. As you probably know Brown Clee is the highest peak in Shropshire at 1722 ft. but did you also know that during the last century it had the highest coalfield in Britain? Indeed it was at that time the centre of much mining activity but has still managed to retain an extraordinary natural beauty. The track is joined by a tree boundary at the lower edge of the field and arrives at a gateway in front of Lower Norncott Farm. Go through this and turn immediately right and through a waymarked gate in a hedge after 15 yards.

Turn left now to follow the waymark around to the right of the farm buildings, cross a driveway to a metal gate in a hedge and enter a field following the left boundary. Cross a stile at the end and continue your line in the next field downhill. If you look carefully there is a waymark on the trunk of an ash tree after about 100 yards showing the direction ahead over a fairly rough patch of ground keeping what has become a more sparse tree boundary on the left. There is a waymarked fence stile hidden between holly trees in the field corner and, once over this, bear very slightly right to pass between two diagonally set oak trees then gradually descend, *slowly* closing with the tree lined brook below.

Keep the line and pass to the left of further oak trees beyond which you can see a gap at the bottom in a crossing boundary. Go through and continue for only about 30 yards before looping right on a path between trees running alongside the brook. After a further 30 yards or so cross a footbridge and a small metal gate onto a lane. Turn left and return to Tugford.

SHORTER WALK

STARTING from the Tally Ho, point 3, follow the main route through to point 5. Turn left onto the lane and continue on it for a little over half a mile as it winds its way through farming communities until arriving at Heath Chapel, point 2. I am sure you will be curious enough to have a look at it (see short note in main text) and, after doing so, pick up the main route again over the dilapidated fence stile and continue back to the start.

Bury Ditches and Clunton

FACT*file*

MAPS: Landranger 137; Pathfinder 930.

DISTANCES: 11½ miles; shorter walks 5¼ miles, 8¼ miles, 7 miles.

MAIN START: The village of Hopesay, 1½ miles north of Aston on Clun which itself is 2½ miles west of Craven Arms on the B4368. There is verge parking available by the telephone kiosk. GR391834

   Public Transport: Very limited bus services 741/742/745/773 from Ludlow (Mon-Fri) and service 748 from Shrewsbury (Mon only) calling at Aston on Clun, 1½ miles south of Hopesay. Alternatively, the train from Shrewsbury stops at Broome Station, half a mile from Aston on Clun. *You will probably find that timings are rather tight for the main walk and you may prefer to do one of the shorter ones, or to start from Clunton.*

SHORT STARTS (pages 94 and 95): (1) The Crown at Clunton, about 6½ miles west of Craven Arms on the B4368 and 2½ miles east of Clun. GR335814. (2) Hopesay. GR391834 (3) Bury Ditches Fort. GR334839

   Public Transport: As above. The bus services from Ludlow (but not from Shrewsbury) also stop at Clunton.

TERRAIN: A challenging walk at any time of the year over one of the most attractive areas of Shropshire, incorporating the magnificent Iron Age Hill Fort of Bury Ditches. *The long walk should not be attempted by less experienced walkers.*

THE PUB: The Crown was recently taken over by a consortium of villagers. It is a small but comfortable local with a main bar, pool room and a restaurant which is popular for Sunday lunches. Ales on offer include Ansells, Tetley, Beamish and Carlsberg together with guest beers such as Great Western Revival and Shropshire Lad. Bar snacks served.

Open 12 noon – 11 p.m. daily except Sunday, closed 3 – 7 p.m.

HOPESAY. *A small but interesting village whose name is derived from the word for valley (Hope) owned by Picot de Say, a Marcher Lord in Norman times. It is surrounded by hills and contains several listed buildings, the oldest of which, apart from the church, is Hopesay farmhouse in the village centre. These together with large well cultivated gardens attached to many of the properties, give the village an attractive ambience with an air of waiting to catch up with the twentieth century. The church of St. Mary is worth a visit – it is of Norman origin although much of the interior owes its appearance to*

Victorian refurbishment, including an ornate carved oak alter screen. An area of adjacent grassland has been transformed into a wildlife sanctuary by a local community group.

TURN towards the church and around to the rear. There is a super barn conversion called 'Sitchfield' and to the side of it bear right along a broad track on the Shropshire Way. Go through a timber gate and an open gateway after another 50 yards into a pasture field with Bank Wood off to the left. Continue forward with a post and wire boundary on your right and follow it round to go through a waymarked gate into the next field. There is a good view backwards from here over Hopesay and Hopesay Hill beyond, which is owned by the National Trust.

Proceed on roughly the same line through the centre of this large field (at the time of research the landowner had left a track to mark the way) with the tree topped Burrow Hill over to the left and at the top the ground levels out and you reach a waymarked gate on your right. Go through this, then bear left through a similar gate to follow the left boundary of the next field. You pass through another gate to the left of an oak tree and, at the top of a rise, go through yet another gate bearing half right across the bottom right corner of a field to a small timber gate on the opposite boundary. *I found it necessary to walk around the edge because of crops.* **1**

Go through the gate and turn left onto a broad track which shortly starts a long slow descent towards the village of Kempton. On a clear day you can see Bury Ditches Fort to the half right with its strangely shaped earthworks which can be examined at close hand a little later. After a while

Part of the ramparts of Bury Ditches Fort

89

you meet and continue ahead along a metalled surface down to meet a junction with the B4385. Here a waymark will inform you that you have been walking along 'Wild Edric's Way'. Edric led local resistance to the Norman invasion and many legends have grown around him. It is said that

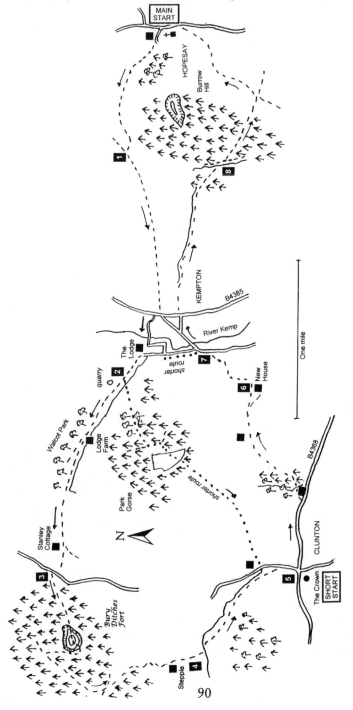

if his ghost is seen riding furiously over the hills it is a portent of war. Any sightings should be reported immediately to the authorities!

Turn right, then left in another 50 yards down a lane between cottages. Ignore a waymark on the right after 75 yards and continue on the lane as it winds right, then left to cross a ford , bends left by some pretty cottages and then turns right to meet a T-junction. Bear right here and go through a gateway by 'The Lodge' onto a track.

Ignore a crossing right of way and follow the track around to the left and, after a further 150 yards, there is a waymarked gateway on your left leading onto a track up to Park Gorse. **2**

Those on the short route will take this left turn, otherwise press on past a small disused quarry, over a cattle grid or a stile to the left of it and through pleasant parkland, still on the Shropshire Way. This section is part of Walcot Park which extends to 1000 acres and contains an eighteenth century mansion built by Clive of India for his retirement. You will pass Lodge Farm on the left after which the track starts to rise more steeply and, after only a further 50 yards or so, veer left along a narrow path in front of a derelict cottage.

The path winds through fringe trees with a stream below on the left. At certain times of the year the adjacent banks are littered with wild flowers. Continue forward at a waymark post up a short embankment to another waymark post at the top where you bear left to rejoin the main track. Almost immediately go through a gate into a lovely secluded valley. After passing through another gate the track loops left but you should continue forward over a stile in front of the isolated Stanley Cottage.

Carry on around to the other side of the cottage as the track weaves between outbuildings and proceeds upwards through a gateway to exit onto a lane. Turn right here then left after 100 yards into the Bury Ditches car park. **3**

A number of routes span out from here including the Jack Mytton Way (a nineteenth century character renowned for practical jokes) and Wild Edric's Way. We need to follow the waymarked 'red' route starting on a path uphill to the right which leads up to the fort. This is a long, fairly steep, climb through pine woods but when you reach the top I doubt whether anyone will consider the effort not to have been worthwhile. Almost at the top is a gateway and a plaque telling you some facts about the fort and you then pass through the original entrance to the fort itself.

BURY DITCHES. *Apparently there are over 20,000 ancient hill forts in the British Isles and this is one of the best of them. The plaque will give you some details which I won't repeat here except to say that this was a major settlement in the first millennium BC and the magnificent defences are still clearly visible. If you bear half right after the entrance you reach a viewpoint with superb 360 degree views through the Long Mynd, Ludlow, Clun, Offa's Dyke, Stiperstones and various other landmarks – on a clear day that is. The fort is now in the care of English Heritage.*

When ready continue on the track along the top of the fort to exit over a stile, after which the track loops right and carries on for about a quarter of a mile to reach a junction with the Shropshire Way. Turn left, enjoy the expansive views to your right over the Welsh borders, and after about 120 yards bear left at a fork following the red marker, then almost immediately right on a grassy path downhill. At the bottom cross a forestry track directly to continue your descent, still with red marker, and you will shortly arrive at another crossing track. Here you depart from the red route by turning right along a path which rises slightly for a short distance then levels out to follow the left edge of the fir covered Stepple Knoll which, as you will see, is being actively managed with felling and new planting.

After a while you meet and continue ahead along a forestry track. This is fairly straight for about a quarter of a mile and, just before it loops right, look for a waymarked stile on the left down into a field. Cross and turn right along the top edge of the field and cross another stile in a crossing fence. This brings you onto a broad farm track which winds left then right and you go over a further stile by a gate then through a gate in front of Stepple Farm. Walk towards the buildings for 20 yards before turning left to pass to the left of them, ignoring a right of way to the right. **4**

You pass through a gateway to join and continue ahead along the main entrance to the farm but only for about 25 yards before bearing right through a gateway into a field. Now bear very slightly left downhill across the field towards the tree line below, to find a stile and gateway in the bottom left corner. There is a well defined track across the field to the same point but this is not the strictly correct line and is there purely for the farmer's convenience. Enter onto a track to the side of a pool which is culverted into a pretty stream on the left which you will now follow most of the way into Clunton.

Once over the culvert veer left into a field and cross a stile 70 yards ahead. In the next, large, field bear half right diagonally across it towards a tree lined knoll – there was at the time of research a narrow path beaten across but this may not always be there. In the top right corner there is a stile to cross into a steep sided pasture and from here follow the tracks ahead parallel with the meandering brook.

Go through a waymarked gate onto a grassy track which actually meets and crosses the brook; however you don't cross it but go over a stile on the right into a field to continue the line forward, still with the brook on your left. At the second waymarked stile ignore the confusing direction right and go straight ahead on the same line to reach another stile after 50 yards which exits onto a lane. Turn right into Clunton and The Crown will not be difficult to find. **5**

You may find the pub more difficult to leave than to find but, on doing so, turn right down the B4368 towards Purslow. There is a footpath for most of the way but care is still required along this road for a little over a third of a mile before turning off left up a waymarked track just before reaching a new timber structure in front of a more traditional house. Cross a stile after 70 yards and bear right into a field following a post and wire boundary on the right heading towards a wood. The way shortly loops left to reach another stile on your right which in turn leads you across a sparse plantation of poplars to a further stile about 50 yards ahead. I hope that nettles etc. do not make crossing this area in summer too problematical. You will need to negotiate a little stream to get to the stile and a few yards after it is a waymark post at a crossing track.

Go straight over through the pine trees following roughly the same line – this is not critical as you will inevitably come out on the other side of the trees at a post and wire fence in front of a field. If you come out at exactly the right point you will see a waymark post but, in any event, turn left in front of the fence and proceed upwards along the wood edge for about a quarter of a mile to cross a stile on the right just where the tree line kinks left. There are good views along this section over woods and hills to the south of Purslow and ahead towards Burrow Hill Fort.

In the field bear half left cutting off the bottom corner in line with farm buildings beyond to meet a crossing hedge boundary. Turn right to follow the hedge and at the end of the long field there are three gates, two on the left and one ahead. Take the latter and continue the line downhill into the next field still with the hedge on your left. Go through a gate at the bottom, where you can see the roof-tops of New House Farm, ignore a track going off right downhill and walk across the field opposite, gradually moving away from the mixed tree boundary on your left and aiming towards the left of the buildings. You will find a stile in a crossing fence – go over this and down an embankment onto what at times can be a muddy track around to the left of the farm. **6**

The track soon loops left away from the farm across a small field at the end of which you go through a gate and continue the line forward in the next, undulating, field to meet a sparse hawthorn tree line on your right. The ground dips quite steeply into a gully and you continue ahead through it, then bear round to the right to join another line of trees going down into a valley with a ditch alongside. Follow the ditch line around as it bears left but, where it kinks sharp right towards a lane, carry straight ahead across a short section of field to a stile close to the bottom left corner which exits onto the same lane. Turn left and after 150 yards there is a narrower lane off to the left leading around the rear of Kempton village. **7**

This left turn is reserved for those on the short route so continue on the lane, over a bridge across the River Kemp and bear right at a fork by farm buildings to reach a junction with the B4385. Cross carefully and go through the gate opposite into a field – do not go over the adjacent stile onto a sunken track unless you want wet feet! Follow the long left field boundary alongside the sunken track and go through a gate in the crossing boundary into another long field, at the end of which bear left through a gap in the hedge on your left and then almost immediately go right over a stile to continue in the next field on the same line. At the end of this field is a waymarked gate and stile set apart. Take your pick and proceed on the same line towards a large wood ahead. On reaching a pine plantation bear left through a waymarked gate and over a stile, then after only 15 yards – just as the path enters a gulley – bear right through trees along the top edge of the gulley. You will pass a waymark post on the edge of the embankment and then another directing you to continue on the same path between an avenue of pine trees. At the end is a stile to cross following a waymark half left down an undulating field, aiming roughly in line with farm buildings ahead nestling in front of the wood. Go over a fence stile in the crossing boundary and continue your descent over a little plank footbridge which you can see below, and then head half right to a stile 50 yards ahead. **8**

Cross the stile and climb the embankment onto a forestry track and turn right, but after only 30 yards bear left up another, more stony track. On meeting a complex junction of tracks, turn left then immediately right after 15 yards along a grassy path leading downwards (there is a footpath sign at the path entrance). The wood ends on the left and you cross a stile to continue ahead to a further stile where the wood also ends on the right. Cross this onto a narrow sunken path which can get boggy. It is probably best to take the narrow path along the left embankment or even walk in the field on the right.

At the end, where the gully opens out at a crossroads of tracks, cross the stile diagonally opposite and onto another sunken path to the right of a field edge – i.e. effectively bearing left at the cross tracks. If this is too wet or overgrown follow the field edge itself. The gully ends and you go through a gateway onto a broad track between hedgerows and, where this ends after about 150 yards, continue forward through a waymarked gate onto a narrower path. This winds around to the right and starts to rise gradually to pass a waymark post on reaching level ground. After a while the houses of Hopesay come into view in the valley below on your right. Proceed now on a broad track as it drops to meet a lane where you turn left back to the start.

SHORTER WALK

From Clunton, point 5, follow the main route to point 7. Bear left along the lane around to the rear of Kempton village where you have the River Kemp for company for a short while and, as the lane loops right, you go straight ahead through a gate to the side of 'The Lodge' onto a broad stony track. Ignore a crossing right of way and follow the track around to the left for 150 yards or so until arriving at a waymarked gate on the left leading onto a track up to Park Gorse. This is point 2.

Go through onto the track but not as far as the wood. Look for a waymark post in the verge on your right directing you right at an angle of about 30 degrees up an area of rough ground. This is a sort of ridged gully and the correct course appears to be along the gully but gorse and trees obstruct the route. However, the line is not critical so find your way to the top of the gully where it meets the wood and here cross a stile and then a forestry track onto a broad earth track opposite.

Climb steeply now with fir trees to your right and beech on your left.

After a while all the trees become fir and thicken. Eventually, after an energy sapping climb, you meet a forestry track and turn left onto it.

Directional care is required now. After 150 yards you pass on the left a broad grassy track going back downhill. Some 20 yards further on, just before the ground levels out, branch right up through the trees on a fairly wide if not entirely obvious path to a stile at the far side.

Don't worry too much if you miss the turning and come to a junction – simply bear right and go through a metal gate at the end of the wood and along the edge of a tree line to reach a stile on your left after 150 yards. If you did manage to find the earlier stile, cross it into a large field enclosed by trees, which I personally found to be quite an enchanting spot. Continue the line forward across the field to a line of fir trees opposite to reach another stile – the same stile referred to if you went the 'wrong' route. Cross the stile into trees on a narrow path for 50 yards to exit via a fence stile into a field.

Follow the descending post and wire boundary on your right with super views ahead and to the left over Soudley Wood, Clunbury Hill and beyond. At the end of the field cross a stile (there is also a stile in the left corner, but ignore that) and turn left to continue your descent on the same line but now with the boundary on your left. At the bottom of this field cut off the very left corner to a stile in the adjacent boundary and cross into the next field bearing slightly right cutting off the top right corner to a further stile after 70 yards.

Cross over the next field directly to another stile in the facing boundary and on into the next field following a post and wire boundary on your left. The descent continues and a good bird's eye view opens up over Clunton on the left. After 200 yards, before the fence line starts to swing right, cross a stile on your left between hawthorn trees into a meadow with a fence on your right. A further stile is crossed after 60 yards, whereupon continue the line forward across the centre of an enclosure recently planted with young trees. You negotiate another stile at the far side and in the next, sloping, field cross towards the left of a cottage below to cross yet another stile before bearing right onto a track in front of the building. This exits onto a lane where you turn left back into Clunton.

ALTERNATIVE SHORTER WALKS

1. Start from Hopesay and go through to point 2. Then follow the shorter route link from point 2 into Clunton before picking up from point 5 through 6, 7 and 8 back to Hopesay. Distance – 8¼ miles.

2. Start from Bury Ditches car park, point 3 , and follow the main route through to point 7. Turn left here and follow the shorter route for a short distance to arrive at point 2. Now continue forward on the main route from point 2 back to the car park. Distance – 7 miles.

18
Hopton Wafers

FACT*file*

MAPS: Landranger 138; Pathfinder 952

DISTANCES: 7 miles; shorter walk 2¾ miles

MAIN START: At St. George's Church just to the south of the village of Milson, about 3½ miles south-west of Cleobury Mortimer on the Tenbury Wells road. GR639728.

Public Transport : Nothing suitable. You may like to start from Hopton Wafers (see below).

SHORT START (page 100): At the Crown Inn, Hopton Wafers on the A4177 Cleobury Mortimer – Clee Hill road. GR637763

Public Transport: Bus service 192/292 Birmingham/Ludlow calls at Hopton Wafers.

TERRAIN: Mainly waymarked paths over undulating countryside. Some of the paths are little used and may be overgrown in summer so this time of the year may be best avoided. Good views of the Clee Hill slopes and no climbs of any significance.

THE PUB: The Crown Inn is a former sixteenth century coaching inn now sympathetically restored into a charming pub with great character. It is a free house and has an enviable reputation for good food, boasting English Tourist Board Three Crowns and Egon Ronay 1994. In the bar you can obtain snacks and choose from a good selection of ales including Boddingtons, Murphy's and guest beers. Beer garden and outside seating. You can even stay the night if you wish.

Traditional opening times.

THE ancient church of St. George is tiny, almost French-like in appearance with a small tile-hung bell tower. The porch and internal roof timbers are partially eaten away by woodworm but hopefully this is no longer active. From the church walk up to the Cleobury Mortimer road and into the village, then bear left along the lane signed Coreley/Clee Hill. After about 200 yards turn right along a path between stone walls, with a new building on the left, and almost immediately pass through a gateway leading towards Oak Farm on a roughly surfaced track.

Continue around to the left of the farm buildings and through a metal gate onto a track crossing a field. This loops right and heads towards a group of trees where you go through another metal gate and over a footbridge. Follow the path left between rows of hawthorn and beech trees and ahead is yet another metal gate to the left of parallel stone walls. Go through this, or over the stile to the side of it, and proceed into a field with the boundary on the right, climbing gently in the direction of Mauns Rough ahead.

On reaching the trees turn 90 degrees left along the top edge of the field where pleasant views open up over countryside to the south. At the end pass through a small metal gate, continuing in the next field with the boundary on your right and through a further gate into another field. The ground now starts to level out and Little Down Farm is visible to your left. Pass through a gate at the end of this field and into the next to reach another metal gate in front of Upper Down Farm. **1**

All this passing through gates and fields sounds a little boring but it's not really – the countryside is very attractive even if the paths can get a little overgrown in parts during the summer. Continue on a short track and go through a gate to pass to the left of the farm buildings onto a track, which on the other side develops into a narrow lane. When you reach a crossroads turn left and after about 200 yards there is a crossing right of way with a stile on each side. Take the one on the right and head down-field with a boundary on your right of mixed trees. There are good views at this point, as indeed there are on earlier sections, of the small settlements nestling on the side of Clee Hill.

At the bottom of the field the boundary curves left and you will shortly see a stile in the trees on your right. Proceed with care down a short embankment, over a brook (no footbridge) and cross the stile before climbing another embankment on the far side into a field. Now follow the field edge rising gently with a mixed tree boundary on your right and, about 50 yards from the top before reaching a lane, cut left slicing off the top of the field through a gateway into the adjacent field.

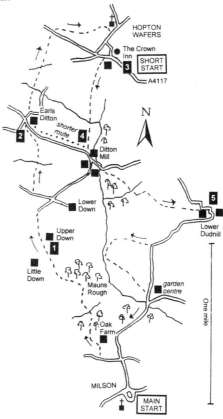

Now follow a course parallel with the right boundary with Earls Ditton Farm further to the right to pass through a gate in the top right corner. Bear left onto a lane and you will immediately arrive at a crossroads. **2**

Bear right at the crossroads between farm buildings

along the lane signed Hopton Wafers and after 100 yards where the lane bears sharp right there are two gates on your left. Go through the right hand gate and cross the centre of the field, keeping just to the right of a line of electricity poles, towards a copse in the dip. Hidden away in the trees is a footbridge but you will need to keep a sharp lookout to find it – the location is about 15 yards to the right of a continuation of the line past the last electricity pole. The footbridge is single plank and the approach can be very overgrown in summer. Once over, cross the stile on the far side and continue in the field directly forward, climbing gradually.

Cross a stile into the next field followed by another stile after which the ground levels out and you reach a small gate and a plank footbridge. Cross this and the ensuing field towards the top left corner where a look back will be rewarded with extensive vistas over the surrounding area. There is a stile in the field corner leading into a small field and on the other side of this a gate which exits onto the A4117. Cross the main road carefully and over a stile directly opposite, and follow the waymark, effectively cutting off the right corner of a field. You will pass through a gate, then a gap in the far boundary to the right of an oak tree and continue into another field, descending gradually with a tree boundary on the left, following a course parallel with the road which leads to Hopton Wafers.

About 40 yards before reaching a right-hand kink in the boundary, branch left through a gap between the trees across the adjacent field to a stile on the opposite boundary. Having negotiated this stile cross the next field directly to another on the far side to the left of a metal gate, heading just to the left of the church. Go over and then through another gate after which bear right into a small field to cross a stile under an oak tree.

The church should now be in view and you continue directly towards it through another small field to pass through an unusual double kissing gate and into the churchyard. Take the path around the church and turn right on reaching a lane to walk through a residential area of mixed period and modern houses. On arriving at a junction opposite the primary school turn left to find The Crown on the junction with the main road. **3**

HOPTON WAFERS. *Derived from 'Hope', the Celtic name for a valley between hills, 'Ton' meaning enclosure and 'Wafre' after one Robert le Wafre who once held the manor. The village was once a hive of industry boasting three paper mills, stone quarries, coal mines and iron workings. Indeed, it is thought that the first blast furnace in the Midlands was located here and there are still a number of sites in the area with remains of these early industries. Today it is just a pretty rural village which has to make do with one pub instead of the earlier two. The church was rebuilt in 1827 and contains a remarkable monument to Thomas Botfield, local benefactor and pioneer of the coal mining industry in Shropshire.*

When you have summoned up the willpower to leave the pub turn right up the main road for a distance of 20 yards or so and bear left along a tarmac lane signed 'No Through Road'. You will pass to the left of a bungalow and continue along a grass track to a stile and onto a sunken path between rows of trees. On reaching a further stile, cross and continue on a path which emerges into an open field where you carry on forward with a hedged boundary on the left.

Where the boundary kinks right cross a stile to the left of a metal gate and descend gradually towards trees. The tree line curves left and you will shortly see a footbridge on the right over a brook. Cross this and in the next field follow the boundary keeping trees on the left. At the far side the boundary loops right and after a further 20 yards cross a fence stile on your left where the tree line ends.

The next field is undulating and you will see below you on the left a water undertaking with huge pipes carrying the water from the Elan Valley to Birmingham together with various little buildings associated with it along the way. Keep the tree line on your right to reach a gate which leads into a newly created caravan site. Continue through the site until reaching a tarmac lane on the far side of it. **4**

Turn left onto the lane and bear left at a fork around Ditton Mill to follow the lane through a pretty section alongside a stream, crossing a footbridge after about 50 yards. The lane now rises between trees and as it bends left look for a stile on your right beneath an ash tree in the hedgerow. The embankment up to the stile is a little steep and can get overgrown, so negotiate with care. Once in the large field follow the waymark across the centre of it and to the left of an isolated tree towards a tree line on the opposite boundary. There you should find a waymark between oaks with a small pool on the right. This leads you down to a plank footbridge and over a stile on the other side into a meadow.

Follow the waymark half left across a rough plantation and after about 50 yards cross a fence stile. Following another waymark go across the centre of the field. At the top left corner there is a crossing farm track – turn right onto it and after 10 yards cross a stile on the left into a facing field. A waymark now directs you half left across the centre of the field. Aim to the left of a clump of trees and when you reach the far boundary there is a dilapidated gate just round a projecting corner exiting onto a lane. Turn right onto the lane to reach Upper Dudnill Farm with its picturesque black and white Elizabethan style farmhouse. **5**

Continue on the lane for maybe a little over a third of a mile, passing Haybridge Nurseries, until it bears sharp left. If you wish you can short cut the walk by carrying on along the lane for a further third of a mile to meet the Cleobury Mortimer road at Haybridge. Alternatively, there is a waymark on the right into a large field taking you over a fence stile and along the right boundary. Pass an isolated oak tree to reach a metal gate in a crossing fence; pass through this and bear left to follow the top field boundary with a brook below.

Immediately before you come to a large oak tree cross a fence stile on your left and then bear half right to walk across the first field, aiming well to the left of a black and white cottage that you can see off to the right until you meet a hedged boundary to the adjacent field. A little directional care is required here. There is a double stile hidden in the hedge which you will find though you may not come across it straight away. Once over the stile, cross the next field bearing slightly right towards a cottage ahead to find a waymarked gateway onto a lane. Turn right, then right again on meeting a junction with the Cleobury Mortimer road. The 'cottage' actually turns out to be a garden centre which sells, amongst other things, ice cream – very welcome at this point on a warm day. Follow the road for about half a mile back into Milson and the start.

SHORTER WALK

STARTING from The Crown, point 3 , follow the main route to point 4. On exiting onto the lane here main walkers turn left but you turn right and continue with it as it quietly wends its way for a third of a mile or so into Earls Ditton, point 2. Now rejoin the main route back to the pub.

Ditton Mill

100

Index

More walking guides from Meridian...

WALKS AROUND THE MALVERNS
by Roy Woodcock
Twenty walks covering the entire range of hills and the neighbouring commons, together with some of the delightful countryside nearby. Distances range from two miles to eight miles, plus a 'leg stretcher' of between ten and sixteen miles (depending on the starting point) that takes in the full length of the ridge and ascends all the Malvern peaks.
ISBN 1 869922 32 8. £5.95. 112 pages. 32 illustrations. 20 maps.

COUNTRY WALKS *in* WARWICKSHIRE *and* WORCESTERSHIRE
by Des Wright
Twenty circular walks that explore some of the two counties' most attractive areas. The walking is easy, mostly on the flat and with few climbs. Distances range from 2½ to 8½ miles although some can be combined to give longer walks.
ISBN 1 869922 33 6. £5.95. 96 pages. 16 photographs. 21 maps.

HEART OF ENGLAND HILL WALKS
by John Newson
The eighteen circular walks in this collection explore a variety of hills in the Heart of England – some well known, others that may be less familiar. The distances of the main walks vary from 10½ to 14½ miles. However, most include the option of a shorter walk and these range between 6 and 10 miles.
ISBN 1 869922 30 1. £5.95. 96 pages. 21 photographs. 18 maps.

WATERSIDE WALKS *in the* MIDLANDS
by Birmingham Ramblers: edited by Peter Groves
Twenty-two walks featuring brooks, streams, pools, rivers and canals. Some can be found a short distance from the centre of Britain's second city; others will take the reader further afield in the West Midlands and into the attractive counties of Warwickshire, Worcestershire, Shropshire, Staffordshire and Derbyshire.
ISBN 1 869922 09 3. £4.95. 112 pages. 28 photographs. 22 maps.

FAVOURITE WALKS *in the* WEST MIDLANDS
Edited by Tom Birch and Mary Wall
A collection of twenty-two attractive walks from members of the Birmingham CHA Rambling Club.
ISBN 1 869922 26 3. £4.95. 112 pages. 24 photographs. 23 maps.

HIDDEN HEREFORDSHIRE
A Book of Country Walks
by Julie Meech
A churchyard awash with spring daffodils, a river bordered with ancient willows, a unique Norman church with comic, grotesque and erotic carvings, a fourteenth century dovecote with 666 nesting places, a Neolithic burial chamber, countless medieval timber-framed buildings, a chance to see the rare Red Kite — these are but a few of the delights encountered in this book of twenty circular walks.
ISBN 1 869922 16 6. £4.95. 112 pages. 21 photographs. 20 maps.

RIDGES and VALLEYS
Walks in the Midlands
by Trevor Antill

A selection of walks within the counties of Shropshire, Staffordshire and the old county of Worcestershire taking in some of the better known, and some lesser known hills; and most with one or two pleasant surprises.

ISBN 1 869922 15 8. £3.95. 96 pages. 12 photographs. 19 maps.

RIDGES and VALLEYS II
More Walks in the Midlands
by Trevor Antill

Following the theme established in the first volume, Trevor Antill describes eighteen further walks in the counties of Shropshire, Staffordshire and Worcestershire. Some of the areas explored are among the lesser known parts of the region.

ISBN 1 869922 20 4. £4.95. 112 pages. 21 photographs. 19 maps.

RIDGES and VALLEYS III
A Third Collection of Walks in the Midlands
by Trevor Antill

Rolling hills, delightful woodlands, charming villages, attractive rivers and fine views are some of the features that readers of the previous two volumes have come to expect. They will not be disappointed with this new collection of eighteen more walks in the counties of Shropshire, Staffordshire and Worcestershire.

ISBN 1 869922 22 0. £4.95. 112 pages. 11 photographs. 19 maps.

THE MONARCH'S WAY
by Trevor Antill

A new long distance walk that closely follows the route taken by Charles II after his defeat by Cromwell's forces at Worcester in 1651. Starting from Worcester it goes first north, then south through the Cotswolds and the Mendips to the coast, then along the South Downs to Shoreham where Charles escaped to France. Visiting many historic places, perhaps previously known to readers only through the history books, it also goes through some of the finest scenery in western and southern England. Each volume is written in sections that also provide a series of attrective day walks.

Book 1: Worcester to Stratford-upon-Avon. 175 miles.
ISBN 1 869922 27 1. £5.95. 112 pages. 19 photographs, 19 maps.

Book 2: Stratford-upon-Avon to Charmouth. 210 miles.
ISBN 1 869922 28 X. £6.95. 136 pages. 21 photographs. 23 maps.

Book 3: Charmouth to Shoreham. 225 miles.
ISBN 1 869922 29 8. £6.95. 136 pages. 21 photographs. 25 maps.

Available from bookshops or, if in difficulty, directly from the publishers. Please send remittance, adding the following amounts for postage and packing: order value up to £5.00 add 75p; up to £10.00 add £1.00; over £10.00 add £1.50.

MERIDIAN BOOKS, 40 HADZOR ROAD, OLDBURY B68 9LA

Please write for our complete catalogue of books on walking and local history.